Charles Bingham

The Game Fishing Year

B. T. Batsford Ltd, London

For Suzanna, Nicola and Lara

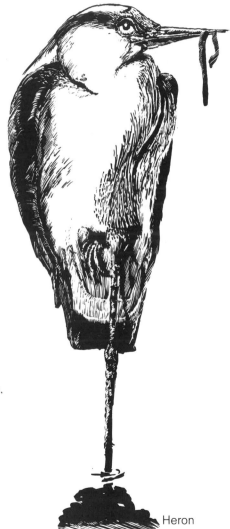

Heron

ISBN 0 7134 5966 2

Typeset by Deltatype Ltd, Ellesmere Port
and printed in Great Britain by
The Bath Press, Bath

for the publishers
B. T. Batsford Ltd
4 Fitzhardinge Street
London W1H 0AH

Contents

Contents

Acknowledgements

I thank the editor of *The Field* for allowing me to reprint *The Survivor* in this book. I also thank John Fogden, who has allowed me exclusive use of his salmon and sea trout water on the lower Dart for many years.

I am indebted to those who have contributed their varied experiences, including: Tony Allen, for his salmon day on the River Itchen; Mark Owen, for salmon and sea trout on the River Ewe; Dr Tom Owen, for an account of his successes on Loch Maree; Bob Sinclair-Taylor, for his splendid salmon double on the River Tamar; The Hon. James Stuart, who helped to thread the eye of a needle for a lady on the River Findhorn.

I extend particular thanks to Mr D. B. McMurray, headmaster of my old school, Oundle, who suggested Julian Waterman as an artist. Julian left the school in 1987 and is now studying at Oxford University. I follow his career as a wildlife artist with eagerness.

I thank the following for supplying photographs: Tony Allen –figs 1, 28, 29, 34, 35, 36; Mark Owen – figs 42, 43, 44; Bob Sinclair-Taylor – figs 60, 61, 62, 69, 70; Noel Swan – figs 20, 21, 22, 23, 24, 25, 26; Jeremy Wastie – figs 17, 18.

To Tony Allen, my sincere thanks for taking me fishing on the Test, producing photographs, tying minute flies, checking my manuscript and, above all, for his company on the river bank.

Finally to my wife, Pamela. Without her patient encouragement I would not have been able to write this book.

Introduction

In the last decade I have been privileged to teach hundreds of people to fish for trout, sea trout and salmon, mainly on three-day courses. Although they have learnt the basic skills in this period, it is impossible to endow them with all the knowledge I have gained by fishing for fifty years.

Overnight they cannot be instilled with that sixth sense which, from the feel of the wind, a burst of bird song which may follow an air temperature rise of two degrees, and a dipped hand testing the warmth of the water, can comprehend an imminent change in fish behaviour. This sixth sense alerts the angler to fish in the right place at the right time and to know which lure to use and when.

I have included my own experience and those of others fishing with me in the eight months from March to October. Additionally, I have described a winter visit to the salmon spawning beds and included two short fishing stories.

The major theme of the book is to set out the types of game fishing available at the start of March and the fishing opportunities from then on. I have included extracts from my diary to explain both successful and failed ventures: the near loss of a 7-lb 3-oz trout from the River Kennet because of a poor net; and the hooking of a much-fished-for salmon after the sun had dipped below the hills at the end of a clear bright day.

Although eight months are covered here, the season is longer in some areas. The salmon season begins in January on the Helmsdale and the Thurso in Scotland, and one can fish in Cornwall on the Camel until 15 December. Many lakes are also open for rainbow trout fishing throughout the whole year. In the region of South West Water you can fish for sea trout on 3 March in some rivers, but not until 1 May in the North West Water region. The brown trout season commences on 15 March in Scotland and 3 March in some Welsh waters. None of these dates imply that the fishing will be productive on these opening days, only that you may legally fish.

This volume is not a step-by-step manual on how to catch game fish (for that I refer you to my earlier book, *Salmon and Sea Trout Fishing*). Instead, it is a yearbook to guide you through the seasonal changes that affect the fishing of salmon and sea, brown and rainbow trout. You will be able to see how a rising summer sun, an east wind, or scudding rain clouds affect the changes in a fish's behaviour. Then, you will be able to anticipate the reactions of the fish and enjoy the memorable catches that will follow.

Glossary

Adipose fin – small fin on the back of a game fish between the dorsal fin and the tail

AFTM scale – defines the weight of a fly line

Alevin – the minute fish which hatches from an ova

Backing – an additional length of strong, thin line joined to, and beneath, the fly line on a reel

Backing up – a method of fishing a salmon fly whilst moving from the tail to the head of a pool

Baggot – a salmon swollen with eggs which it cannot extrude

Bail arm – the part of a fixed spool reel which gathers and winds the line onto the spool

Bank – (*in boat fishing*) an area of shallow water in a loch

Bass – a bag made of woven reed for holding and transporting fish whilst keeping them cool and damp

Beak hook – the point is slightly turned in towards the shank which may, or may not, be sliced, for worm fishing (*see* **Sliced hook**)

Blow line – (also known as floss line) undressed fluffy line blown out by the wind to carry the dapping fly away from the boat

Bob fly – the fly closest to the butt of the leader, and thus the fly line, when a team of flies is being fished

Butt – (*of leader*) the thickest part of a tapered leader where it joins the fly line

Butt – (*of rod*) the handle end of a rod

Buzzer – an artificial midge nymph

Caddis – another name for a sedge fly

Chironomid – a midge

Dangle – (*on the*) position of fly, or taking salmon, when straight downstream of the angler

Dropper – a second or third fly fished on a leader between the point and bob flies

Dun – first aerial stage of flies of the order *Ephemeroptera*

Finnock – a small Scottish sea trout

Fish – the term usually refers to a salmon rather than a trout or sea trout

Flopy – a French rubber plug bait

Fry – a small young fish (*after the alevin stage*)

Gaff – a pointed, barbless hook on a shaft for landing salmon
Gape – defines the gap measurement between the point and shank of a hook
Gillie – person with detailed river knowledge, employed to help an angler
Gravid – (*hen*) fish with well-developed roe, sometimes dripping from the vent
Grilse – a 'one sea winter' salmon of about 4–6 lb
Groyne – man-made protrusion from river bank to create a salmon lie or enable the angler to cast over inaccessible water
Gye net – a salmon or sea trout net carried on the back

Hopper – term used by West Country salmon netsman for a grilse

Kelt – spawned fish
Kype – upward hook on lower jaw of cock fish

Leader – (*cast*) the length of nylon joining the fly line to the tail (*point*) fly
Ledger – *see* **Paternoster**
Lie – place where fish rest in river
Lure – wide term embracing spinning baits, artificial flies, plugs, etc.

Mend – to move the fly line on the water after initial cast by switching upstream or downstream to decrease or increase the speed of passage of a fly across the river to the angler's bank
Mepps – a revolving spoon bait

Neck – (*of a river pool*) the narrow entrance where the river runs in to the pool
Nymph – underwater stage in life cycle of some insects

'On the fin' – position of feeding river trout close to water surface and waiting to take floating natural flies
Otter – device to release spinning baits caught on the river bed

Parr – small fish, only a few inches in length, in the early stage of life cycle
Paternoster – (*ledger*) method of fishing a spinning bait, worm or prawn slowly and close to the river bed
Peal – West Country term for a sea trout of any size
Peal sling – quick-release harness, of leather or webbing, by which a Gye net is carried on the angler's back
Piling – sheets of metal or wood to reinforce the bank of a river
Plug – an artificial vaned bait, usually fish-shaped, sometimes jointed, which darts, dives, rises and pops about underwater when retrieved by a spinning reel
Ply – a river is 'in ply' when colour, height and temperature of the water are suitable for catching salmon
Point fly – the fly at the end of a leader
Priest – a short truncheon with which to kill fish by hitting on the head
Pupa – an immature stage of some flies

Rapala – a type of plug bait
Redd – depression cut in gravel or small stones by fish in river bed where female deposits ova, which are then fertilized by milt of cock fish

Glossary

Run-off – the downstream, tail end of a river pool

School peal – small sea trout on first return to river in summer from the sea

Scissors – (*to be hooked in the*) description of the point of the angle between the upper and lower jaws of a fish

Sea lice – suckered lice found on flanks and back of salmon and sea trout when they enter the river from the sea. Denotes a very fresh fish as they drop off after two or three days in fresh water

Sea trout – a migratory brown trout

Sewin – a Welsh term for a sea trout

Skate – (*skid*) a fly crossing the river, or drawn across the loch surface, in or on the water surface film

Sliced hook – type of hook with barbed shank used in worm fishing

Smolt – an immature salmon or sea trout migrating down river in spring to make first entry to the sea

Spate – the rise and fall of the water level in a river following rain

Spinners – general term covering revolving artificial baits

Spinner – (*natural fly*) second aerial and final egg-laying stage of flies of the order *Ephemeroptera*

Split cane – a rod of hexagon cross section formed of six faced strips of cane or carbon bonded or wrapped together with silk

Spoon – a type of artificial bait, sometimes revolving

Stale fish – a salmon or sea trout which has been in fresh water for some weeks, usually a fish in autumn that is darkish or red

Stickle – a shallow section of river between two pools

Tail fly – *see* **Point fly**

Tailer – a wire noose to land salmon. Grips at wrist above the tail

Toby – a type of spoon bait

Trace – about a metre of nylon between the swivel at the end of spinning line and bait

UDN – ulcerative dermal necrosis

Walking up – a method of persuading a hooked salmon to move upstream

Wye weight – a weight used in salmon and sea trout spinning and bait fishing; metal loop at one end for line attachment and swivel at the other to which the trace is knotted

Wind knot – a knot formed unintentionally in the leader whilst casting. Weakens the leader

CHAPTER 1

MARCH

The month of the greatest angling prize – a spring salmon. This fish is likely to be heavy, strong and silvery in the early weeks of river life after entry from the sea. Additionally, in March, one may stalk wild brown trout on a few rivers if the water is low and clear. Rainbows may be pursued in the lakes, with a sinking line on cold days and a floater in warmer weather. Success usually coincides with spells of clement weather. These are early days for trout, but the pleasure of the renewed freedom of the waterside and release from the housebound hours of winter is undeniable.

March rookery

Consider spring salmon, examining landings and losses, near losses, and the reasons for success and failure.

Opening day on a salmon river

The salmon season on my home river, the Dart, opens on 1 February. The season in some waters commences in March or April, sometimes as early as January. 1 March, when my game fishing school season begins, is a good month to start, for there are a few salmon in the rivers and the daffodils are in bloom on the bank. Very few people learn to fish in February, but let me start with the opening day and a short entry from my diary for the year 1981.

1 February. Dart. A 10-lb salmon taken on our side in Nursery Pool on opening day

That salmon may be described as a 'creeper'. It is doubtful whether there is a period in the year when salmon do not enter a river, even if it is only one or two isolated fish a month in the winter. These salmon often hang about in the lower reaches, creeping up a pool or two at a time, and are usually mopped up by the rods in the first few days of the season. So if you are free, go to the river on the opening day.

Landing a salmon in fast water with a tailer

23 and 24 March 1974. River Taw. Rising Sun. Tony lost a fish above Crockers on a No. 3 Mepps on Saturday. Sunday he took a fish of 12 lb at 12.30 pm in Upper Rocky on a 2-in. Black & Gold Devon minnow. Murch had one at same time. I took a fish in tail of Otter at 4 pm, 2¹/₄-in. Black & Gold. Sea lice. 16 lb. Tony waded river at 2 ft 1 in. to tail it for me.

Why couldn't I tail that fish myself or, for that matter, land it in some other way – perhaps by beaching? Look at the scene. Otter is not a pool, it is a fast run with a lie midstream. Casting from upstream of the lie the angler may fish from the right bank where there is a small standing place. This foothold is narrow and was about two feet above the water when I was fishing. Downstream one cannot go far when playing a salmon, for the banks slope precipitously into deep water. Upstream, the water shallows but the bank is still steep. Thus the fish cannot be taken up the river and it is impossible to move up or down except on this foothold strip, which is about 10 yd long. In short, the water rushes by below the bank, and there is no indentation or slack water available.

I had a tailer with me and, at first, with the rod in my left hand, I tried to draw the salmon up the river level with me. It was impossible to keep this heavy fish up with my left hand and also bend to slip the tailer on with my right hand. As I tried to do so the salmon was swept down river. Instead I tried to draw him up to the top of my ten yard strip, take two rapid steps down river and tail him before he drifted back. Again, the salmon was swept away before I could do so. By this time I was worried – it was increasingly possible that the hook would work loose or the exhausted salmon would be washed downstream, from where it would be too heavy to be pumped up by the rod against the flow without the tackle breaking. At this stage, Tony walked up the far bank, saw my position, waded the river at some risk, joined me, took the tailer and had the fish on the bank in no time. It was a near thing, for the hook fell out when the salmon floundered on the bank.

That tailing, which had been impossible for one, was readily accomplished by an assistant. There is no sure way of landing salmon in such places, the gaff being illegal, other than to fish with a companion.

Losing a salmon in fast water with a net

The occasion when I lost a 10-lb salmon in March on the Dart in 1977 is similar to the above incident, but in this case I was fishing by myself and carrying a 22-in. Gye net.

Fishing down a fast run, I cast over to the far side to let the metal Devon minnow swing deep across the river below me. About ten yards down the pool there was a soft thump at the bait, signifying a fish. There is no mistaking the feeling. I moved back up the pool again a few yards and fished down on him a second time – he took. The first fish of the season, I thought.

Only when the salmon began to tire did I realize my hopeless netting position. I had misjudged the strength of the water flow and could not hold out the submerged net against the strong current. Being on the right bank the rod was in my left hand with the butt inside my left thigh for leverage. In this way I could lever the salmon up the river, but each time I extended the net with my right hand the river current swept the net into the bank. The fish then wallowed down river (the worst position for a hook hold), with me hanging on, and then he came off the hook.

In retrospect, I should have realized that landing a salmon in such a place would have been difficult. Over-confidence, or slackness, caught me out. There were two solutions – both difficult but just possible. I could, with luck, have drawn him up through 50 yd of torrential water to a small slack area and beached him. Alternatively I could have taken him down over 100 yd and through a gorge to a deep, dangerous pool. During such a passage, the fish might have snagged. However, I should have attempted one of these plans.

The lesson to be learned is to examine pools and runs *before starting to fish*. Decide in advance on the course of action to be followed if a salmon is hooked and note any beaches, backwaters or indentations in the river bank where a salmon may be landed. Look particularly for an area of slack water where a fish will lose direction, will not be helped by the current and may be netted whilst it flounders.

Relative temperatures of water and air

*9 March 1968. Welsh Dee. Uncle Kiff's water. River temperature 40° F. Air 50°
F. River low and clear. Hooked a fish and rose another on a 2/0 Thunder &
Lightning with a floating line.*

There are two lessons to be learnt from this. The first is that when the air is
substantially warmer than the water, even though the latter is as low as 40° F,
salmon will rise to take a fly close to the surface if the water is clear enough for
them to see the lure. The river level should also be on the low side.

The second concerns the loss of the fish. A proportion of salmon will always
come unhooked, but this one came unstuck owing to the failure to drive home
this heavy iron.

The action came about as follows. To begin with, that salmon just touched
the fly – a well-known feeling like a leaf brushing the lure. Three or four casts
later he took and I gently led him upstream whilst backing out of the river. The
salmon swam on past me and then the hook fell out.

My mistake was to not 'strike' him – that is, to give a good strong lift to bend
the rod to thump in a large hook. In those days I was gentle with salmon, not
liking to stir them up so early in the fight. I still fish this way now, but the fine-
wired treble hooks available today just slide home into a firm hold. Not so the
large single – it must be driven in at once, preferably on the first occasion the
fish is swimming away from the angler. Give a good hard pull when the fish has
its tail towards you – if the hook then slips it is likely to drop back into the
scissors.

Concerning Devon minnow mounts

*21 March 1968. River Torridge. Huntingham Beat. Water 1 ft 10 in. 4.30 pm.
14 lb. Lower Boat Pool. Fish knocked the minnow and came again to a second
cast. 2½-in. Yellow Belly Devon. A metal minnow is better than wood – it
fishes deeper.*

It is 20 years since this event but the lesson I learnt from it has always stayed
with me.

I was spinning in Lower Boat Pool when there was a splash under some trees,
suggesting a kelt. Then another splash in the same place five minutes later.
Clean-run fish (ones travelling upriver on their way to spawn) will sometimes
lie with kelts – at any rate it seemed a likely place to which to cast a minnow.
After the third throw there was a knock, a bump at the bait – quite different, as
many will know, from touching the bed of the river or a rock.

I tensed and cast again, to be taken at once. This was no kelt, I knew, from
the power with which it moved up into the pool. The battle to land him went on

Daffodils

for some time – it was a tricky matter leaning down over some wooden boards to reach the salmon and in those days I used a tailer (now discarded for the net). At last he was on the bank and there was the treble, just inside the lower jaw. I took out the hook at once, and no one on the river that March had better luck, undeserved as well, for the wire mount had almost parted from the treble hook.

Beware eyeless trebles in which a wire mount is laid along the shank, turned back between the hooks to lie again along the shank, where it is whipped down with silk. In this case, the hook was just inside the lower jaw, which has fine teeth along the edge. These teeth had cut the silk and almost freed the hook from the wire. This is not the only risk – the silk may rot too. It will take you only a few minutes to make your own mount with an eyed treble, a swivel and plastic coated wire. Another straightforward arrangement is to take the nylon of your trace, pass this through a wooden Devon with a tulip bead at the tail, and tie direct with a Tucked Half Blood to a ringed treble.

Spinning – on treble hooks, minnow sizes and stiff spinning rods

An entry from 1966:

Taw. Rising Sun. Proprietor – Stewart. Water was 2 ft to 1 ft 10 in. on these three days. 15 March. Beat 5. Water temperature 47° F. Air 56° F down to 47° F by 5 pm. 9¾-lb fresh run with sea lice. Sandpits Run. 4 pm. North wind. 1¼-in. Silver Blue Devon. 16 March. Beat 6. Water 48° F. Air 57° F staying at 57° F through the day. Lost a fish in Crockers 3.00 pm on No. 2 Mepps. At 5.00 pm took fish in same place 9¾-lb. 2-in. Silver Blue Devon. No wind. 17 March. Beat 7. Water now clear and 48° F. Air 56° F. Sunny. Fly and minnow tried and fish risen Upper Rocky. Cost of 2 nights and 3 days about £15. Fishing included in this £3 a day. By the records most fish were taken in first half of March at about 4.00 pm and a few between 11.00 am and 1.00 pm.

There are some useful pickings to be gleaned from these entries, starting with 15 March.

Anyone who knows beats 5, 6 and 7 will be able to visualize that the river was at an excellent height, not in flood (over three feet), not low, just right. The first item of note is the 1¼-in minnow. That is very small for March, but clearly not too small for a water temperature of 47° F. A high temperature for the time of year warrants a small bait.

In addition, the air was warmer than the water, the temperature of which must have risen during the day. A water temperature rise at these levels makes for good fishing, particularly after lunch and at teatime in early spring.

Finally, the diary notes that the air dropped to 47° F by 5 pm. Such a drop is typical of the season, and when the air temperature falls back below that of the water, the salmon usually just shut down for the night. As to the 9¾-lb salmon 'fresh run with sea lice', here is knowledge to be stored. Umberleigh is seven miles from the salt tidal waters at Barnstaple; as sea lice drop off after two or three days in fresh water, the salmon had swum that distance in that time. This is not remarkable, for salmon and large sea trout often cover twice that distance in the same period. It is not unknown to find salmon carrying sea lice twenty-five miles from the sea, when a spate has aided them and the water is warm. Salmon do not run far against cold water.

In March when the water is cold it is not much use fishing for fresh run fish beyond ten miles above the sea in the period of, and immediately after, a spate. From May until the end of the season, if this be October, this distance may be doubled.

For the entry of 16 March, there are several useful points regarding the loss of the salmon in Crockers at 3.00 pm on a No. 2 Mepps. First, the conditions were clearly good for the time of year – warm water and still warmer air. The time of day when both of the fish were hooked bears out the general expectation that two-thirds of fish taken at this time of year will come after lunch. But why was the 3 o'clock fish lost on a No. 2 Mepps? There were two reasons: a soft, fine wire hook on the small Mepps; and too stiff a rod in my hands. Both faults were caused by lack of experience, but also, in the case of the rod, lack of a deep purse.

To begin with, the rod was of tubular steel and designed for pike spinning. I had bought this rod from the Army & Navy Stores, just after the war and used it for pike fishing as a boy. Several years later, I used it for salmon spinning but, lacking knowledge, I imagined a stiff powerful rod would be required for the legendary salmon and so shortened the top by 12 in. Resultingly, the rod became so poker-like that the tackle inevitably snapped and I lost salmon on two occasions. In the first instance, I lost a fish when fishing from a boat just below the junction of Loughs Conn and Cullen in County Mayo in 1955. In this case I used a 20-lb braided line on a multiplying reel and a 10-lb trace at the end of the line. The combination was fatal. The only salmon hooked in the ten-day holiday rose from the depths, took the minnow and turned down. I raised the rod and '*ping*' –the nylon snapped. Such moments are engraved upon the mind and never forgotten.

On the second occasion I had learnt one lesson and changed over to a 16-lb nylon trace. However, I had not changed the hook and was still using the same rod. After the hooking, I thought to myself 'You've strong tackle. All is sound. Make short work of him.' In fact, he had short shrift for me, for as I applied power to the outfit, the hook just bent out.

I therefore learnt that the only solution is to cut off a suspect treble, fit a split ring and attach another treble of the highest quality.

There is still more to be gleaned from the record of that day. The second fish of 9¾-lb was taken *from the same place* two hours later. Do not imagine that when a salmon has been taken from a lie no more may be expected – quite the opposite may be the case, for that lie is clearly agreeable for salmon at that water height. The disturbance caused by playing your fish matters little if the lie has been allowed to remain undisturbed for as short a period as 15 minutes after landing the first victim. Fish are not upset by another being played, *provided that you remain out of sight.* It is by no means unusual to see one pike follow another that has been hooked, and I have twice seen a salmon swimming behind the fish being played. Many times during an angling life two salmon can be taken from the same place within a matter of two or three hours. Don't forget that fish are moving up the river all the time if the water height is right, and a favourable position may be re-occupied within the hour if there are enough salmon in the river.

Now look at the 2-in. Silver Blue Devon. It is generally accepted that as the water level drops and clears, you should use a smaller minnow if the water temperature remains constant. Yet in this case I used a 2-in. Silver Blue to take a fish when I had used a 1¼-in. in heavier water the day before with success. Quite the wrong way around! The lesson to be learned is one that should stay with you – you never *know* with salmon!

17 March

All was fine on this day in respect of air and water temperatures, and the presence of salmon. The spate, however, had gone, and I speculate that few fish would have been taken until the next spell of rain. Success often follows correct timing of visits to the river –all the advantages are with the local anglers. In my own case, in Devon, the river is 30 minutes by car from the house. To time my visits correctly, thus avoiding futile journeys, I have put a dustbin lid outside to serve as a rain gauge; when it is full, I know the river probably is too.

Pitfalls of advising other anglers and relative merits of different spinning baits

A diary entry from 1971 – again on the Taw at Umberleigh.

21 March. Beat 5. Water 3 ft 7 in. in morning. Dropped to 3 ft 4 in. and cleared quite a bit by afternoon when I took an 8¹/₂-lb fish with sea lice. Took right below me half way down Horestones. 2¹/₂-in. Yellow Belly Devon.

and:

24 March. Beat 6. Water 2 ft 7 in. 13 lb. 3.30 pm in usual place in Crockers. No. 2 Mepps with heavy hook. The water is still too high at 2 ft 7 in. for most Beats.

Habitués of that water will know that the river is very high at 3 ft 7 in. Too high for hope, was the general consensus among my fellow guests at breakfast. A friend, Roger, was due to join me that day from Southampton, a journey of at least 150 miles, so I 'phoned him to save a wasted journey. I then went to the river with a 'better be fishing than not' attitude. By late afternoon, the river had dropped 3 in. and cleared a trifle; I took a fish, played and landed it and knocked it on the head. Roger, undaunted by my advice, arrived just as I was bending over the fish to take out the hook. It was very embarrassing.

Rises and falls on a full river can, therefore, be rapid, and an opinion may require revision in six hours' time. Never suggest to a friend who wishes to fish that it is not worthwhile – once again, you never know with salmon.

On to the 14 March and another indication that 'after lunch is best'. Note that the No. 2 Mepps now has a heavy hook which enabled the 13-lb salmon to be played out without mishap. The salmon came from the usual place, a much favoured lie well suited to a Mepps. This lie is on the right side of the river towards the tail of the pool where it widens, and as the water is deep there, the current is slow. Mepps spoons revolve rapidly and are suited to slower portions of a river; if fishing in the fast necks of pools they tend to revolve too quickly, create great water resistance and thus be difficult to retrieve. It is better to use a Devon minnow or a Toby for spinning in fast water.

1 *A flying treble is ideal for landing a salmon on a Toby*

Rusty traces

6 March 1975. Hampshire Avon, Somerley. Beat 3. Joined Bill for lunch and had about 6 casts with his rod. 2½-in. Yellow Belly. Hooked a fish 1.00 pm, Bill played and I gaffed. 15 lb. A nice clean fish about 100 yd above Ellingham Bridge.

The minnow and trace had been made and used for mahseer (a large, freshwater fish) in India many years previously by a friend. In the above incident, the wire of the trace was rusty and broke during the fight, but by the most extraordinary chance the wire caught on the barb of one of the trebles and wrapped itself around this hook. No doubt, the wet trace had been put into its tin and been left to rust. Avoid these risks by drying your baits in the airing cupboard on returning home from fishing, and making your own mounts from plastic coated wire which will not rust.

Colours of Devon minnows

26 March 1975. River Test. Broadlands. Beat 1. Oak Tree Pool. 3.00 pm. 12 lb. 2½-in. Yellow Belly. Very clean silver fish. Water high and a bit coloured. Bill gaffed.

After lunch again! Notice that bait was a Yellow Belly and the water was slightly coloured. Anglers of experience have their own preferences on the colour of a minnow best suited to particular river conditions. Mine are as follows. A Yellow Belly is the best colour for heavy dirty water; a Silver Blue should be fished as this coloured water clears; a Brown & Gold or Black & Gold are telling shades in the peat-stained water draining off a moor.

'The second time down'

4 March 1979. Dart. Lost a fresh fish in Middle Run whilst following Richard Hobbs down the pool. 2-in. Silver Blue Devon. 5 fish taken so far below Buckfastleigh. Saw two more fish on 6/7th March.

There are those amongst the salmon angling fraternity who say they prefer to fish a pool after someone else has had first crack. Do not believe them! All the same, the angler who goes down second, or even third, has a good chance even if he follows at once, provided the preceding angler has not frightened any fish in residence. Fish are unlikely to be scared when a spate is in progress, and the number of times salmon have been taken behind me and by myself casting after others is greater than I can remember. At the same time, if with a friend, your chances are increased if flies, spinning baits, depth of fishing and perhaps speed of retrieve are varied between the two of you. If fishing with my daughter we sometimes agree that she precede me, by fifty or one hundred yards, casting a 1¼-in. Black Dart tube fly. I would follow with a 1 or 1½-in. Hairy Mary. These tube sizes are, of course, dependent on the water conditions. Or one of us might fish down with a floating line and the other follow with a sink tip or sinking line. The many combinations give a wide choice: Yellow Belly and Red & Gold Devons; Blue & Silver and Black & Gold; a Devon followed by a Mepps or Toby. You could fish down with the fly and the other then back up.

There are so many small variations in the manner of working the fly by different people. Some let the fly progress in little jerks; others say, with a twinkle in the eye, 'it's hard enough for them already – you mustn't make things even more difficult for the fish by jerking the fly about'. Those with this attitude ensure a steady movement by the lure.

Natural conditions will also change the fishes' behaviour: a cloud covering the sun; a gust of wind arriving to ripple the surface; a shower. I remember a particular occasion when I was teaching a group of four boys. It was late in the afternoon, we had worked all day up and down the river, fished all the pools many times. Depression and disbelief had set in when there was a heavy shower which lasted only 15 minutes. A shout erupted from one of the boys who had flopped his fly idly into a small pool covered many times already. Stimulated by the rain, a salmon rose and took – the boy was so astonished that he hung on tight; the salmon leaped once and bent out the one hook of the treble by which it was held, before the boy could collect himself.

Kelts

8 March 1979. Dart. 7¹/₂-lb salmon on No. 2 Mepps. 2.30 pm. Also returned a kelt. Both in Rookery Pool.

Be sure you know the difference between a kelt and a fresh salmon. This is only a problem for the novice who has caught neither. The kelt is a spawned salmon (or sea trout for that matter) which will be about two-thirds of the weight of a fresh fish of the same length. Most salmon kelts die, but some attempt to return to the sea in early spring, travelling down river at the same time as springers are coming up. At times kelts are, therefore, caught when you are expecting something better. By law, you must return kelts to the river; be sure to wet your hands before removing the hook from one or you will burn its skin. Put it back into the river, holding its head to the current until it recovers and swims away.

The first indication that you have hooked a kelt is when a fish gives up to the rod quickly, since kelts are not strong. In addition, the back and belly of a kelt are parallel whereas on a fresh salmon the back and belly are convex to each other; the vent of a kelt may protrude; and the head is over-large in relation to the body. Don't be fooled by the colour – many kelts are silver and as such are known as 'well mended'.

Baggots

14 March 1967. River Taw. Fox & Hounds hotel. Water 2 ft 4 in. on gauge on arrival. Roger had fish 11 lb in Oak Tree on Beat 6 at 11.00 am. 3-in. Yellow Belly. Water coloured.

This 11-lb salmon ought not to have been killed, but I knocked it on the head myself as follows. I was fishing several hundred yards below Roger, who had not caught a salmon in his life. The railway line is on the far side of the river, and that morning a ganger came running down to me waving his arms and shouting that Roger was into a salmon. I dashed up stream to see the exhausted fish wallowing in the river, with Roger some feet up on the bank. It struck me at the time that the salmon looked an odd colour, being rather a light brown;

however, we carried on, tailed the fish and examined the catch on the bank. I knew that the fish was not fresh run but by then there were three railwaymen on the far side who shouted in unison 'Knock it on the head'. Still I hesitated, looked at Roger, miserable at the thought of losing his catch, and then I resolved the matter with a swift blow.

Examining the fish, I could see it was very like a salmon that has been in a river for some months – rather coloured and full bellied. We put the salmon on the hotel slab, where it looked dreadful alongside a fresh fourteen pounder, and then got into trouble with the River Board bailiff who pronounced that it was a kelt. Later, he added that he would overlook the matter as it was Roger's first fish and we didn't know any better. Later, when cleaned, I found the salmon was full of well developed roe which it had been unable to extrude for some reason – it was a baggot.

A change in the weather

11 and 12 March 1972. Taw. Rising Sun. Spent weekend with Bill. River 3 ft and 2 ft 10 in. Very cold east wind. No fish. Day after we left weather warmed up and guest had 3 fish on Beat No. 5.

Almost certainly, the very cold east wind had made the air colder than the water. The wind, being dry, would have also cooled the river surface further by evaporation. When such conditions change for the better, and mild rain comes out of the south west, go to the river at once, for a water seemed empty may yield a harvest as it warms. A similar situation arises in winter in a river holding pike – after a prolonged spell of ice, frost and snow, go to the river when the thaw commences. Many times in January I have caught several pike from the Dorset Stour near Wimborne on such a day, particularly if the sun comes out after lunch.

Lies, fixed spool reels and water level gauges

14 March 1981. Dart. The largest salmon I have seen taken from our beat. 20-lb exactly by Dr Tom Owen on an ancient 1½-in brass spoon. 4.00 pm in tail of run below Rookery Pool Tom's first salmon, netted by Mike Allsop, on their first day of salmon fishing instruction. Total below Buckfast now 17 fish.

From the above incident two lessons were learned by the anglers; and information was later obtained about that salmon's life cycle. We removed some scales from the flank of the fish and sent these to South West Water for them to read the growth rings under a microscope. The report came back that the salmon had spent two years in the river before migrating to sea, followed by three years' marine life before returning to the river on the spawning run. The three years of rich marine feeding were the reason for the heavy weight. As a matter of passing interest two-sea-winter salmon in the Dart average 9 lb, and one-sea-winter fish, called grilse, weigh between 4 and 7 lb. The grilse go to sea as smolts in April, or thereabouts, and return from June onwards the following year.

But notice where the salmon was caught—'in tail of run below Rookery Pool'. If you have fished that beat you would know at once that the water was high for a fish to rest in that tail or, rather, if you knew the water was high, then it would be sensible to fish the pool tail. In fact it is only worth fishing that lie in high water, there being insufficient depth at lower levels. The exact resting place is only 2 yd wide and 2 yd long in a river 25 yd across. The favoured place is in front of a line of sub-surface rock which stretches out to three-quarters of the river's width. In high water salmon will generally be caught in the wider splays and quieter places at pool tails. In low water pay attention to pool necks where the rushing flow provides cover by bubbles and turbulence, and there is a good supply of oxygen in summer.

Tom was using a fixed spool reel which I had provided. I was not present during the battle, being down the river with another pupil, but arrived just after the fish had been grassed. Tom remarked that he had found the reel 'fiendishly difficult'. Since then, I have carried a vivid picture in my mind of a wallowing, surging salmon and Tom winding the handle of his reel 'like a fiend', unable to recover the line because of the slipping clutch! An amusing situation for the onlooker but one that is easy to remedy for the angler. To play a salmon on a fixed spool reel it is necessary to set the clutch so that the salmon can just pull out line.

When the salmon has drawn line from the reel and then stopped running, the line must be recovered and the salmon drawn closer. It is no good winding the handle whilst the spool clutch slips and clicks, for no line will be retrieved and each unavailing turn of the handle revolves the bail arm three or four times around the static spool and *each revolution puts a twist in the line.* Instead, put your finger on the spool to stop it slipping, raise the rod tip almost vertical – that is, pump the salmon towards you – and then wind as you drop the point of the rod. Repeat as necessary. The fixed spool is versatile, being suitable for the heavy baits of March and the light lures of summer. It is less expensive than a multiplier and is less liable to line tangles because the spool is static and cannot over-run.

You might be interested to know that the nylon monofilament reel line was 18.7-lb breaking strain and the trace 15 lb. It is not necessary for the trace to exceed, or be as great as, the weight of the fish, for the latter is supported by the water.

On arriving at the river, it will be obvious from a glance whether the water is at a high or low level and, of course, you will have an idea of the likely state before you arrive, from recent rainfall. All the same a water level gauge will indicate exactly which lies will be at a good height, those for which there is too

2 *In March an ideal river height to catch salmon is between the top lip and the centre of the pipe at the right side of this picture. Here, however, the level is suitable for peal fishing at night.*

much water and others where the level is insufficient, without your needing to walk along the river to look at each place. These three levels may come within a water height difference of one foot – so it pays to know the position accurately. On my beat on the Dart, adjacent to the place where the car is parked, a large land drain of 36-in. diameter is sited in the opposite bank of the river. I pay no attention to the water coming out of the pipe, unless it is muddy, when a few imprecations are appropriate, but look with close attention to the river level in relation to the pipe mouth. If the level is over the top of the pipe it is too high to fish; from the top to half way down, the high water lies are worth a try; from half way down to one quarter up, the low water lies; if level with the bottom, go home! In the summer the water ought to be four inches below the bottom of the pipe for good sea trout fishing. The water level on Tom's day was high, with water washing around the top rim of the pipe.

More on salmon lies and water heights

*23 March 1982. Dart. Bunny Bird had his first salmon. 14 lb. Sea lice. 4.30 pm.
2-in. Brown & Gold Devon. Half way down Carradon Turn Pool.*

3 *Salmon caught in medium water* (23 March 1982)

and:

26 March 1983. Dart. Len Norton-Wayne took a fish of 9½-lb in high water in tail of Carradon Turn Pool on a 2-in. Yellow Belly Devon. 4.00 pm.

4 *Salmon caught in high water* (26 March 1983)

In a picture I have of Bunny and his wife, Joanna, holding that fish whilst standing on the right bank of the river, it is just possible to make out the water level pipe behind them. The river is half way up the orifice. This means the water is at a *medium* level, and therefore it is logical that the salmon came from a lie *half way down* the pool.

In the second incident Norton Wayne's fish was hooked in the *tail of the pool* in *high water*. I can visualize the moment now, for the salmon at once splashed. I leapt to Len's side and together we 'walked up' that salmon away from the danger of the pool tail.

I have only once taken a salmon from the neck of Carradon Turn Pool, and that was on 2 May on a 1½-in. Brown & Gold Devon thrown upstream in low water.

Note that both these March salmon were, once again, taken in the late afternoon. It is also interesting that the fish taken on the 2-in. Brown & Gold was at a medium water height. The high water fish took a Yellow Belly – almost certainly the higher river would have been more coloured, and in such conditions I suggest a Yellow Belly shows up best.

Smolts

Salmon spawn in mid-winter in the headwaters of their rivers. The eggs hatch after about three months and the development stages of alevin, fry and parr take place over a period of two years' river life until the fish is in the region of 9 in. in length. At this stage the young salmon takes on a silver colour and migrates down river to the sea. These immature salmon, known as smolts, have a voracious appetite. On their seaward journey down river in March and April they will snatch at, and take, the spinning baits of the early season salmon angler. One is at once struck by the size incongruity of these happenings – the 9-in. smolt taking a No. 3 Mepps or a 2-in. Yellow Belly intended for the 10- or 15-lb mature salmon entering the river at that time. The smolt makes a good job of its attack, to the extent that it may engulf the entire treble hook, although the bait itself will be too big to go in its mouth. Of course, the smolt must be recognized and returned to the water. There is not much difficulty about identification because it is likely to be the only silver 9- or 10-in. fish in the river at that time – a small sea trout kelt of 12 oz is quite close in size, but it is not as brightly silver as the smolt and is plainly flabby in the body. To release the smolt is often a problem for the mouth will literally be filled with hooks. Now is the time to make use of those artery forceps we all ought to carry. Each hook may be gripped with the forceps in turn, and the struggles of the little fish will usually bring about release. Try to carry out the whole operation under water, and don't handle the fish unless imperative. If it is necessary to hold the smolt, be sure to wet and cool your hand in the river for a full minute before doing so.

Smolts are met frequently in April as well as March, but I, personally, have not come across them in May. The duration of the journey to sea will vary from river to river, as will the timing. Lift your hat to the departing smolt and wish it well – it is next year's grilse or the salmon which you hope will come your way in two or three years' time.

Rainbow trout – fly depth and air and water temperature

Rainbow trout have no close season; you may therefore fish for them throughout the winter. This is because they breed in the wild in few locations in

5 *Three rainbows taken on Black Muddler. Total 10 lb 8 oz. Newhouse Fishery, Devon* (20 March 1987)

the British Isles. On instructional game fishing weekends in early March I usually include a day or two at rainbows at Newhouse – a small lake in South Devon. There is little fly life so early in the year, in fact almost none if the water is cold and the air even colder. In consequence, the trout stay deep and that is where the angler must fish, and fish slowly, with large flies scratching the bottom of the lake. By fly I mean a lure: this is not an insect imitation, for my choices are dressed with a red, orange, yellow or black wing and a striped body. It is the same principle as early season salmon fishing in cold water – deep fishing to lethargic fish with a large bait.

At Newhouse in March I instruct anglers to cast out a long sinking line, and then count ten to let it go down before starting their retrieve. If a count of ten does not trip your fly up on the bottom of the lake try fifteen and then twenty. Finally you will hit the lake bed – then, next cast, reduce your sinking time by five. Back you tweak the fly, and the trout attach themselves unseen. It's all very simple and rather uninteresting, but the trout make a good supper.

On 29 February 1984, at Newhouse, George, Bill and I did just that – fished deep and slow. We were rewarded by 7 trout weighing 11 lb 7 oz. And the lures? George used red or orange creations of his own. Bill used a Worm Fly, a useful fish catcher in the early season. The worm fly looks like one brown creepy crawly with a red tail, set on sex, following the tail end of another! One feels that fishing the worm fly is not quite the done thing – but after a long fishless winter one needs results.

The next day, 1 March, we returned to the lake and the diary reads as follows:

George, Bill and 'self. 18 trout. 24 lb 3 oz on a fine warm spring day.

Nothing very remarkable about that you may think, but I have a memory like an elephant's and those fish were caught on flies fished off *floating lines.*

Arthur Wood, the original master and innovator of floating line fishing for salmon, or greased line as it was then called, wrote:

'Many people seem to think that surface fishing is no use, except in shallow water and during hot weather. Experience has shown me that it is equally good in icy water as long as the air is warmer than the water.'

This was written between the wars. Wood later added:

'The lowest temperature at which I fish greased line and small fly is about 39° or 40° F, but if there is a very cold wind I use a big fly and sink it.'

Few of us fish for trout in water temperatures below 40° F in March, and it is a fair supposition that the water on our day was above that level. It matters not, for the air was warm, it was fine and we felt the advent of the release of spring in those clement conditions.

Wild brownies in March

Have you ever wondered where the small wild brownies are in early spring?
River trout fishing for browns commences in many areas in March. On the 15th
of that month in the south west you may take to the hills, moors and combes
with a wet or dry fly on your point. That is your right. The trout have other
thoughts. If you can find them in any numbers in March, and catch them on the
fly, please share your secret with me!

All the same there is a chance with a wet fly as the entry of 20–21 March 1982
verifies:

Bob, Mike and John caught four brown trout on wet flies on the Lyd and Dart

And so, a wet fly it should be. Fish down or up, it doesn't matter, but upstream
casting, with a little time allowed for the fly to sink as it drifts back to you, will
work the fly deeper. As the trout are clearly not rising to surface flies they must
be somewhere else and that can only be closer to the river bed. So try a No. 12
Black & Peacock Spider, tied by yourself with a twist or two of lead wire under
the bronze peacock herl body.

Many are the warm March days when I have sat by the river at lunch time and
I have given thanks for seeing another spring – the sun on my back and a dram
of the Scottish wine warm my soul. The warmth brings on a hatch of olives,
which drift down the river, in single file, blond tissue wings erect and tiny tail
whisks curving up – and not one trout acknowledges the generosity of the river.

CHAPTER 2

APRIL

On the first day of April fly fishing for trout commences on many lakes and reservoirs. The catches, which may be numerous, are predominantly rainbow trout since they are quicker growing than brown trout and, therefore, less expensive to stock. Some of the trout taken may have over-wintered in the lake. Most will have been introduced by fishery managers during the final week of March. These 'stockies', as they are called, are hungry, and in many waters there is little natural food available in the water in early spring. The result of these two factors, together with the inexperience of the fish, ensures heavy catches for anglers on opening day.

Dipper

It is all too easy, unless the weather is unhelpful, and many limit bags will be taken – some even before breakfast! These bonanzas are achieved in most cases by long distance casting with a sinking line, and a lure tied to the end of the leader. Sometimes the temperature is warm for a day or two, resulting in a chironomid (midge) hatch; trout may then be taken on a small No. 16 or No. 18 Black Gnat. Some anglers may be unable to see their minute fly at a distance, or even to tie it to the leader – for them there is the solution of fishing the midge nymph, a buzzer as it is called, just below the surface.

April is a lean month for trout fishers on most rivers owing to lack of fly. Anglers of long standing on a beat, the patriarchs of the parish, shake their heads, grumble, and agree that 'the fly is not what it used to be'. They may be right, but who can blame a fly for deciding not to hatch into those cold inhospitable days which often comprise early April?

Apart from a few hefty specimens, sea trout are not yet about in any number, nor will be for a couple of months. A few large ones may take a salmon fly or spinning bait as they go up river.

The month marks a change for the better in salmon fishing. Not in numbers of fish perhaps, but in method. River temperatures rise to a level which warrants fly fishing with a floating line, and smaller flies are likely to come into use. The spinning rod may be hung up in the back of the tackle cupboard until late autumn or the following season. The floating line, or a sink tip, may be used from now on almost without exception until the end of September, and good catches will continue with this method on warm days until the end of October. You can make a start this month on the most rewarding, memorable and enjoyable ways of taking fish. The floating fly line, maintaining the fly 3 or 4 in. below the water surface, brings salmon up from the river bed into view – the experience is heart stopping. A river skin bulged, stretched and broken by the black back as it curves over and then recedes from view; the white rimmed mouth swallowing water and the fly; the tail which waves a momentary goodbye and at the same time signals that the time has come to raise the rod.

Reservoir rainbow trout – to cast with or against the wind

On the whole, it is profitable to cast against the wind when fishing for trout from a reservoir or lake bank. This is due to a number of factors, not the least being that waves disguise fly line flash in the air when you false cast; waves also break up the surface tension outline of line and leader floating on the top. In addition, the drift of surface water will take trout along with it to the side to which the wind is blowing. Surface food will also be carried there, and it is not unusual to

6 *Landing a trout* (15 April 1987)

7 *Cleaning the trout* (15 April 1987)

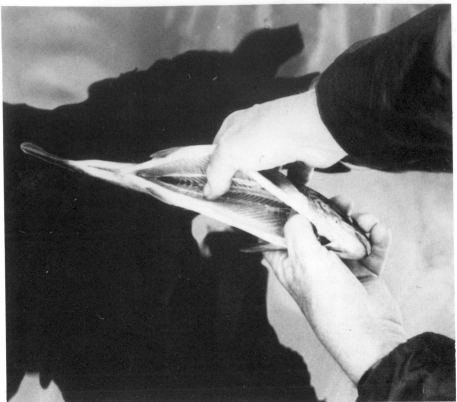

7a Run your thumb down the backbone to clear away the blood

find a band of grey midge pupa cases several inches wide along the shore at water level. If taking a day's fishing at a strange still water it is not sensible to fish only in those places clearly frequented by local anglers – they may decide to cast with the wind because it is easier. Instead, ask which way the wind has been blowing over the past few days – then go to the bank to which it has been blowing.

To cast against the wind, you will need a stiff rod of 9 or 10 ft in length. The rod must have the power to move a heavy line fast, and thus with more momentum than would be achieved with a light line. This momentum will enable the line to cut into the wind, particularly as the rod throws a narrow loop. Anyone using a soft trout rod will be unable to fish effectively against the wind – the line will not cut into the gusts owing to a wide casting loop, and being lighter, and slower moving, it will have less momentum. So, take a stiff rod with you, preferably of carbon fibre. These rods are narrower in the tube than fibreglass and split cane, are lighter, and being thin have less wind resistance when punching out on the forward cast. It is more effective and less tiring to cast into a stiff breeze all day with a carbon fibre rod than one made of either of the other two materials.

15 April 1983. Tamar Lake. Our first warm trout day. We cast against the wind on the far side near the dam. Nick had four rainbows. Edward, Francis, Alan and myself shared seven more. Total 11 rainbows, 14 lb 14 oz. Best trout 1 lb 10 oz. 10 on the Whisky, 1 on a Sweeney Todd. All taken deep, although fish also taking buzzers on the top.

Not only did we cast against the wind but we also fished close to the dam. In reservoirs, it is often productive to fish at one end or the other of the dam wall if the prevailing wind is blowing to the dam. A good harvest is almost assured if the wind arrows into the corner between one end of the dam and the adjoining bank. That is where we were, in the south east corner into which a rough north west wind was blowing. It may be that trout drift down the lake with the wind, come to the obstruction of the dam and then swim along its length to the corner. That is where you have the best chance of catching them!

A final comment on: '*All taken deep, although fish taking buzzers on top*'. As we could see the trout rising, surely we should have fished for them with floating lines? Should we not also have used dry Black Gnats or a buzzer nymph? To do so would be rational. The trout were feeding, why not add to their fare? To this I can only reply that when trout are intent on tiny flies, when they are all rising to them and also eating the fly nymph as it hangs in the surface film, they will often ignore your imitation of the natural. Perhaps it is because there is so much food to choose from. Perhaps your fly is a bit too large. By all means try your best to take them by imitation. If you fail, and the trout will have nothing to do with you, take your courage in your hands, use a sinking line and large lure, leave the risers to it, and seek the denizens of the deep.

The following year, 1984, on 3 April, again at Tamar Lake, Gavin, a

Raven

13-year-old boy caught a rainbow on a Black Buzzer, whilst Jeremy, his friend, took two more on the same nymph and another two on a Pheasant Tail Nymph. Next day these two nymphs brought us nine rainbows, totalling 7 lb 4 oz. However, according to my diary the wind was in the south east which was behind us. This certainly brought the calmer conditions more suited to a small nymph than the rougher adverse wind of the previous year. The Pheasant Tails would have been on No. 12 hooks; the buzzers smaller at No. 14 or No. 16.

Near the surface or close to the bottom? The level to fish is anyone's guess if the trout are 'nymphing', although I would probably start with a floating line. If one method does not work try the other, but always change a losing game.

The colours of trout wet flies and lures

The entry of 15 April 1983 records the trout as having fallen to Whisky and Sweeney Todd lures. The wing and body of a Whisky are orange in colour; the body is ribbed with gold. The Sweeney Todd has a black body ribbed with the striping of silver tinsel and the added inducement of a bright red throat hackle. These two lures successfully attract trout by arousing their curiosity and aggressive instincts.

Fish see in colour, with the red end of the spectrum making the greatest visual impact: red, orange and yellow. The attention of fish is also caught by striped items. Both of these lures have these attributes. Neither is an attempt to imitate an insect – they are just attractors, as are salmon flies. The two lures also have to be large. We use only Nos 8 and 10 long-shanked hooks in these patterns, because their use is confined to the cold waters of April and late autumn, the rough gales of summer, and deep fishing on a sinking line in heat waves.

The most successful traditional wet flies, in use for a number of generations, were designed before fish vision was very well understood. By luck and experimentation some got it right! The best examples are the Peter Ross, with its black and white stripes of teal flank feathers for the wing, a silver and red body ribbed with silver, and the black and orange tail of golden pheasant tippet fibres. Also the Black Pennel with its black, silver-ribbed, body and golden pheasant tippet fibres for the tail.

Novices hooking a trout

Tamar Lake. 1 April 1982. Opening day. John caught 2 rainbows and 1 brook trout. Jim, his first 2 rainbows. Myself, 3 and 1 brook. Total 7 lb. Jim demonstrated the new method of landing trout called the fully flexed rod method, which requires no net. We hope to see this system widely adopted for speed and keeping your feet dry.

You never know what beginners will do when they hook their first trout. If you are by his or her side you can instruct them. If you are a hundred yards away, there is no telling what will happen. One thing is certain – they will forget almost all they have been told about playing and netting fish in the surprise and speedy action of the moment. Jim just wound his first, which would have been about one pound, up to within a foot of the rod tip where it dangled like a carrot. He then swung the hapless trout ashore, dumping it on the grass. Who complains at success?

When casting out from the bank at a lake and then retrieving the line in short draws, the rod tip is usually held close to the water surface. The length of the rod, being horizontal, points at the trout, which takes the fly and hooks itself against the direct pressure of the line held over the rod hand forefinger. When the pull is felt the angler should raise the rod at once so that, when near the vertical, it acts as a spring and absorbs the shocks of the trout's escape attempts. Novices are often so surprised that they leave the rod in the horizontal position where it cannot flex. A violent shock from the fish may then break out the hook hold or snap the nylon. Breakages also occur when the trout makes a sharp dash, pulling down the rod tip, and then jumps with the tackle already under tension. Keep the rod up, give line, tire the fish and take your time. Sooner or later it will surrender.

River dry fly – brown trout and salmon parr

23 April 1980. Dart. Caddaford Ford. Louis caught his first brownie on a Kite's. There were a great many salmon parr rising to a hatch of Grannom.

8 Fishing upstream dry fly on Dartmoor

The Kite's Imperial is a first class imitation of the Large Spring Olive (today sometimes named Large Dark Olive). This member of *Ephemeroptera* is common on the lower Dart in March and April on warm days. The hatch takes place from noon onwards, and thus Louis's choice was acceptable to the trout.

As to the Grannom, this is an early season daytime sedge. They usually appear in considerable numbers and may be recognized by their grey colour and the small green egg sac at the end of the female's abdomen. Anglers may have different experiences to my own, but I have not found the trout take them avidly – salmon parr evidently enjoyed them on that day. Salmon parr must be distinguished from small brown trout – they are only 5 or 6 in. long and must be put back. The trout has a thicker body than the parr, which has a distinctly forked tail and clear anal and adipose fins. The adipose fin of the brown trout is orange, red or black, and there is an opaque whiteness to the leading edge of the anal fin.

In any event remember to handle the parr with respect. They are delicate fishlets who return after many months' marine excursion as robust salmon. Take care of them by bending in the barb of the fly hook or fishing barbless. Above all, if you have to release one, wet and cool your hands in the river if it has to be steadied during release.

A trout hooked in the dorsal fin

25 April 1980. With Bill and Louis. 4 rainbows. Total 4 lb 6 oz. 2 on Pheasant Tail Nymph in light northerly breeze. An elderly fisherman from Okehampton, and his attendant non-fishing wife, were close to us. At noon he hooked a large trout which jumped once or twice. After 10 minutes his wife came along the bank to ask me to play the fish as her husband had recently suffered three coronary attacks and was becoming faint and breathless. I found the trout hooked in the dorsal fin by a very small nymph on fine nylon. 50 minutes later we landed the trout, which weighed 4 lb 4 oz. Both delighted; had a drop of Scotch from his bag.

The foul hooking of trout, and particularly salmon, arouses controversy and passion, and rightly so. There are those who would have all foul-hooked fish released – do not argue against that view for it is honest. For myself, in that case, the fine nylon and small hook put the odds on the trout and I am glad I landed the old man's prize.

The perils of one person playing a salmon and another netting the fish

2 April 1985. Dart. Rookery pool. 4.30 pm. Water 47° F. 19-lb salmon. 2-in. Black & Gold Devon. A day for Andrew Livingstone to remember. A good

*number of fresh fish taken in last three weeks below Buckfastleigh in our
area. Most of a large size: 15–22 lb.*

9 *19-lb salmon* (2 April 1985)

I was helping Andrew's mother retrieve her minnow from a tree, when Andrew
hooked his salmon two or three hundred yards upstream of our position. In fact
my glance had just been torn from a salmon lie close by where a tail of broad
shape had momentarily cut the river surface as a salmon slid into position to
occupy the place. Derek, who catches more fish than most of us and is ever
ready with a helpful hand or word, ran down the opposite bank. In agitation
and excitement, he pointed upstream whilst twirling an imaginary reel handle.
Upstream we went, galloping over the rocks and tree roots, and trampling
uncaring on the yellow trumpets of the wild daffodils. I need not have hurried
to Andrew's well-curved rod, for he was as cool as a cucumber, even though it
was his first salmon!

We walked the fish upstream, handing the rod around bankside trees, one
hand to the next. In time the salmon tired. 'Heavy fish; nearly cooked,' called
Derek from the far bank as the salmon, still mid-river, showed a silver side. All
was going well. Andrew now led the fish towards a bank indentation where I
slid into the river in my waders with a 22-in. Gye net. 'Lead him upstream, turn
him, then swim him down head first into the net.' After a while, Andrew did
just that – then we nearly lost him! The salmon's head was entering the net
mouth when it was suddenly drawn out. I managed to take a grip on the tail
wrist with one hand, pressed a finger or two of the other into the gills, lifted him
up, out and onto the bank and sat on Andrew's prize. The cause of all this

undignified turmoil was the lack of co-ordination between rod and netsman.

If netting a salmon for someone else, it is essential that the 'rod' can keep the net in view. He then knows the exact second to slacken the pressure so that the rising net may engulf the fish. Andrew was directly behind me and thus, unable to see the final state of play, did not drop the point of the rod. I should have told him in advance, but there are a lot of things to think about at such a time! There are occasions when it is helpful to have a friend net your salmon, particularly if fishing from a high bank, but you put a responsibility on that person. On the whole, it is best to enter the river to do the job yourself. The whole business is readily accomplished if you are down at water level. Of course the size of net is crucial: small nets only accommodate small fish. The net we used on that day had a ring of 22 in. in diameter. Both 24 in. and 30 in. are now available and many choose the middle size. A 30-in. net is a bit too big to carry up and down the river.

Two days later success came for Andrew's brother.

4 April 1985. Dart. Between Tom's Run and Rookery Pool. 12.30 pm. Water 49° F. 14 lb. 2½-in Yellow Belly. Joint effort by Alisdair and self. 2 more fish caught this day at Buckfast.

10 *14-lb salmon* (4 April 1985)

Alisdair was walking up the river with me earlier in the morning when this fish slashed above a well known high water lie. We tried for it as, we later discovered, Derek had done an hour before our arrival. The fish ignored us and went doggo – we might have been casting over barren rocks. Rookery Pool, the Nursery and the runs above occupied us for the best part of a couple of hours. On the way back for lunch we tried again. To reach the lie one casts from a submerged rock promontory. If the water, when standing there, is up to your knees, then that level is just right for the lie – and so it proved in this case. It gave us a sharp tussle in the heavy river but was netted in a small backwater.

How often have you seen a salmon move, fished for it with care, been refused and then, later, plotted its downfall? Many times, most of us would say, perhaps not understanding why. Warmer water; shadow instead of sun; a shower all may play a part. Above all, persistence is most important.

Wild brown trout of Fernworthy on Dartmoor

This reservoir of 76 acres is the Devon equivalent of a Scottish loch. There are heathers and plantations of mature fir trees. Wild tough cock pheasants call from the scrub, and ducks are silhouetted against the sky. Herons fished the bogs and the South Teign river when bronze age skin-clad men peered up the misty, rain-swept valley from the dark interiors of their boulder huts. Their stone circles are now below the lapping waters, except in times of drought when the receding water is sucked away to feed a modern town. You breathe clean air alone and assimilate the centuries at Fernworthy.

It is fitting, therefore, that the earliest activities in this book should have taken place there, in April 1950. In that month I fished the water for seven days between the 13th and the 22nd. The first two days were blank, for the wind was cold as it often is up there in April. The other five days yielded seven brown trout and a sea trout smolt. Four 8-in. browns were returned. Those are the statistics. The flies were all fished wet: Peter Ross, Butcher, Black Pennell, and a Coch-y-Bondhu on the bob. The leader was of knotted and tapered gut sections to a 4X point, soaked over night in the hotel bedroom wash basin. The casts, as they were called in those days, were taken next day between damp felt pads in a copper cast box, where they remained supple and ready for use. The dap, as well, was tried from the boat, following experience in 1949 on Loch Maree. The Dartmoor trout did not take a leaf from the book of their Scottish brothers –they did not appreciate the dap.

Trout of that size are still there. They spawn in the feeder streams where shoals of fry may be seen as they dart for cover under the rocks and boulders. Today, you may not fish for them in April, and rightly so, for at 1,050 ft above sea level the water is cold and the trout will be better in May and June.

On the 22 April 1950 we caught the sea trout smolt on a Peter Ross in the pool below the dam over which cascaded shining pearls of spray. He must have been spawned in the streams above the dam before it was closed in 1943 – since then he had been a prisoner until a chance wave lifted him over the sill. Nowadays, trout sometimes follow his example, being washed over the dam in spring when the water is high and the wind is in the west.

April salmon – sinking lines replaced by floaters

22 April 1961. Dart. 12½ lb. 3.00 pm in heavy rain and high water on large low water Hairy Mary. 23 April. 15 lb. 1.00 pm. High water and still raining.

It was wet and windy on those two days at 950 ft above sea level. Even so, those salmon were taken on a greased line, a leader of 10-lb Fog nylon in a camouflage colour, and a low water fly. With hands wet, white and stiff from the rain, I backed up the Hairy Mary and stripped it in across the tails of two long rough-waved pools. I still remember the first salmon – he came up from the deeps so fast that most of him was visible as he rolled over and took the fly down.

The two fish were looked at later with some interest in the hotel kitchen, and some pondered on how I took them. On the evening of 23 April I sat in the bar with the water bailiff, Swifty Warne. Swifty wore patched leaking gum boots and rode a motor cycle; he ate little but enjoyed a pint, and lived by himself in a cottage over the bridge. He looked as sparse as his thin drooping moustache, and one felt that square meals did not rank high in his order of life. Yet his stern exterior was deceptive – he never arrested anyone, 'just gave 'em a fright an' moved 'em on m'dear'.

Clearly, the success of the two salmon had caused some speculation amongst the locals at a time in early spring when fish were few and far between. Swifty looked at me over the edge of his tankard, wiped the froth from his moustache, and acted as spokesman: 'Zum zay you baint fishin' right, but I do tell 'em you be greasin' th' line. 'Ee be fishin' right, I say. I zeen 'im. Tidn't feasible, they hold, to grease th' line. But I tell'd 'em you be fishin' proper.' Swifty swallowed some beer. 'You'm welcome to our county m'dear.' I was a 'furriner', coming from over the county border in Dorset. He had clearly been embarrassed by the silent accusations of the others, who thought I had used a worm – this being a fly-only water. But Swifty was right; all I had done was greased the line or, to be more accurate, reduced the depth and increased the speed of the fly.

In those days fly lines were made of silk. To make them float you greased them with a product named Cerolene.

April is a month of change in salmon fishing, in particular with the fly. In these weeks, when the water warms up the salmon become more active and no longer stay close to the river bed. They start to rise up to meet the fly in April. Consequently, there comes a day, with the water temperature in the region of 45–48° F, when you may add the floating fly line to your methods. This does not mean to say that in these April days there is no place for the sinking fly line and the spinning rod; they still have their moments, but you may use them less and less. In fact, from the first warm April spell, many fish the floater almost exclusively for the remaining months of the season.

The Wickham's Fancy trout fly

20 April 1984. River Lyd. We had 3 brown trout on Wickham's Fancy.

The river Lyd runs off the western slopes of Dartmoor, through Lydford Gorge, and then on for some miles to join the River Tamar. On the way, it passes below my house. The trout are small, active, well spotted and *hungry*, particularly in the early season. It is a swift stream running first over granite in the upper reaches, and then the bed is formed of smooth grey slate. As with most fast waters there is only a very moderate supply of food for trout. If brownies have no steady supply of food, particularly if in waters which are acidic, they will take what comes and quickly too. They just have time to grab before the current whips the morsel by or another trout seizes the chance. Wasps in season; bees and grasshoppers; the August daddy long legs; the succulent sedge of summer; or the green caterpillar, descending on a silken thread – all are appreciated. Even the mouse and shrew should swim and hug the bank with care; a friend found one in a bulging 8-oz Lyd brown trout not half a mile upstream.

The Wickham is well suited to this situation for it represents no known natural fly. Yet it is a killer in almost any fishery – river, stream and lake – and at any time of the year. The grayling of the Test fancy the Wickham in October and it accounts for rainbows in the reservoirs. The Wickham has a long season, and in the above incident worked successfully in April.

On that 20 April we used the fly on a No. 14 hook tied to a knotless tapered leader with a 5X point. Although 6X would be the best, 5X is fine; 4X is too heavy on the Lyd. On any clear granite or slate-based water where the trout are small use fine nylon. A 4X can be used on the chalkstreams but not for little wild Devon browns. Your equipment need only be the simplest: just the fly and floatant to ensure the hackles dance upon the stream. A little grease for the 4 or 5 ft of leader closest to the line, and a pair of waders. You don't need a net – these troutlets may be beached on a sandy bank. A rod of 8 ft is ideal, particularly if you have to fish beneath a canopy of trees.

Now let's consider the method. The trout have their preferred stations. Often, like salmon, they lie in front of a stone or boulder, or a yard or two ahead of the place where a pool shallows out in an underwater sandy bank. Enter the river, keep low, creep upstream and pitch the fly a foot or two in front of his nose. You must set the hook like lightning with a flick of the wrist – and then he'll fight like mad.

It all sounds so simple, and yet there is a problem which, from time to time, defeats us all – namely, drag. Where water currents differ in speed relative to each other, the main run stream from the steadier sides, your fly may drag. To avoid this use quick casting, a short line and short swim on the surface, then rapid lift off before the current catches hold. Fishing on the Lyd is not particularly restful!

At one period I fished a little Dorset chalk stream, the Allen. The river is about the same size as the Lyd but has a placid bountiful nature. Food for fish is plentiful; crayfish abounded in those days, and pike had to be trapped. The Wickham worked there too – all through the season. We didn't wade the Allen, for there was deep mud in places; instead we fished on our knees from the bank, picking out the dark shadows of the trout through polarized spectacles. April is early for the river, but there was a doctor who let me fish between the watercress beds at Wimborne St Giles. You could buy a great bunch of watercress tied up with raffia in those days, as round as a cider flagon at the cut-off base. The cost was only one shilling and sixpence, which included the small black water snails trapped between the stems. You will never eat better trout with watercress than those brownies from the Allen. In the 1970s, three of us fished the river lower down where it runs through the Crichel estate. Chub, cruising in the shadows, sometimes took the Wickham; opening their thick white lips they sucked it down and then, in startled terror, dashed for cover under the far bank. They soon gave up, those chub, being a rotund fish of small courage.

Yet, as I have written, April days are early for dry fly, for the wind seems to have a habit of arriving from the cold east for days on end. In such conditions, the water remains low and clear, whilst the trout flash like grey arrows across the light cream colour of the chalk river bed at the passing of a shadow. Under these conditions it is well to keep low and a yard or two back from the edge of the river.

April river trout on the wet fly

8 April 1983. Lyd. James, Neil, Jason and his father. We caught 9 brown trout on upstream wet and dry flies, and cooked the fish at the river in the Abu smoker.

On the chalk streams, where fishing on some waters may not start until May, upstream dry fly is the rule. Perhaps a nymph may be allowed later, in July, to help the downfall of well-educated trout. These rules are right and proper in their place. If you want trout meat easily there is always the fish shop slab. The purpose of going fishing is the challenge, the difficulty, the anxiety, and the deception of the trout. It is not a tranquil sport, as sometimes supposed; indeed the participants, at times, may feel a need of tranquillizers! In the West Country and the north the trout are hardy, wild and able to look

11 *Brown trout from the Lyd taken on upstream wet fly* (8 April 1983)

after themselves. Very few are stocked, for these innocents would be welcomed by the heron, the mink and the now returning otter. In these places, the angler may need a little help on the many miles of natural streams, unimproved by the hand of management. That help may be in your fly box already – the wet fly.

You may fish the wet fly upstream, retrieving faster than the current gliding by, or cast down river. It was the upstream wet fly which produced some of the trout for the boys on 8 April. I had had no success early in the morning when demonstrating upstream dry fly fishing, but one of the boys tried all the methods he could think of to come up with the answer. He took a No. 14 Greenwell fly, the wet variety with backward sloping wings, cast it upstream across an intervening fast flow into the slack on the far side of the river. His retrieve, and the drag of the current, whipped the fly down and across in a fast curve – and the trout came with a rush. They had to! What they imagined the Greenwell to be, no one could say, but they were taking their chances on it being food. None of the trout were large, half-pounders perhaps, but mostly six ouncers. We killed nine, and these, when cooked, produced four or five mouthfuls for each of us. We gutted the fish by the river and examined the stomach contents in a saucer – nymphs, caddis cases and beetles were all washed apart and identified.

If you do cook by the waterside there are a number of small portable fish-smokers on the market. They are described as smokers, but we rarely add the oak dust under the grill wires, just using the box as an oven to bake the trout.

On most rivers you can place the box on a bank free of vegetation without the risk of fire. A small tin with a loose wick is filled to the brim with methylated spirits, placed under the box, and lit. When the meths is exhausted the trout are cooked. We carry all our culinary requirements to the river inside the box itself: a flat medicine bottle of meths, a box of matches, salt, and a knife and fork. If there is more than one to dine then you can all eat with your fingers.

The wet fly may also be fished down and across. This is not so readily accomplished and successful as might be imagined. For a start, the angler is upstream of and higher than the trout. He is thus more visible than when casting up the river, and also more likely to pull the fly out of the mouth of the fish than when striking from behind, from which position the fly may be pulled back into the scissors of the trout's jaws. Despite these disadvantages, many anglers fish down, but generally with a longer line and more slowly than the upstream method where a rapid retrieve is essential. There is now no need for a floating line, it being better to sink the fly a little, so far as the lifting current will allow this to be accomplished. March Brown, Greenwell, Butcher, Peter Ross are all good patterns and have their day.

On 5 April the following season a boy called Gavin caught 'a good brown trout' in Abbot's Mead on the Dart on a March Brown. Gavin just cast down and across, let the March Brown swing over in the current, and a 13-oz trout hooked itself and gave him a tussle before being netted. There are always a number of encouraging brownies rising in that pool in April if the river is not in flood, and they give notice that the trout season is upon us.

More to fishing than catching

In April so much goes on at the waterside, be that river, lake or loch. The warden of Tamar Lake tells me that the house martins take midges over his water on the North Cornwall/Devon borders in the final week of March. Certainly, they are there when his fishing season opens on 1 April. Not long after this, if we are picnicking in South Devon a swallow may zig-zag up the river valley. The swallow attracts me more than the house martin, although I am very fond of the little brown sand martin which burrows out the sandy river bank to nest in the dark seclusion of his tunnel. The swift arrives later in this country, about the first or second week of May. He has divided loyalties, nesting in crevices in buildings and being just as happy at dusk screaming up the straight streets of a town as flying high above the water meadows. The swift is a noisy bird who drives away the house martin. At one time we had seventeen house martins' nests under the eaves of our farmhouse, and one pair of noisy swifts in a hole in the wall. Eight years later no house martins remain but four couples of swifts have found crevices in which to nest.

Of kingfishers, there are two or three on our beat of the Lyd and I was pleased to see a nest made in the upturned bole of a tree blown over in a gale.

The heron is a controversial bird – some cannot grow fond of the heron,

12 *The first trout of John Furze's life. Tamar Lake* (24 April 1987)

although he must be admired for his size and the delicate smoke blue of his feathers. At no time of the year is he welcomed on a stocked fishery, least of all in spring when he has young to feed for he is an early nesting bird. The heron will eat almost anything: frogs, young birds, mice and fish. We have a heronry not two miles away from which, some years back, they decimated my early stocking of 12-in. brown trout. I do not stock trout these days for the herons grew fat at my expense. The wild brownies which abound know how to care for themselves better than trout from a protected stew.

A bird of the faster river is the dipper and April is his nesting month. They are always busy, bobbing up and down on the boulders in the river and then flying fast and low up the valley, over the pools and stickles, to a nest built of moss under a bridge. A welcome sight, but particularly this month as a reminder in their nesting activity that this is the time of regeneration.

There is also the moorhen, which always seems to be disappearing into cover and rarely coming out. No doubt they see us first and set off to hide, seldom coming out until we have passed. There are fewer of them now than 40 years ago and this may be due to the spread of the mink – of which we have too many. As school boys we collected moorhens' eggs from their nests in the rushes of the River Nene whilst paddling from lock gate to lock gate in a canoe. We did not do this as vandals or collectors but because we were hungry during Hitler's war, and an egg was an egg.

A duck which prefers fresh water is the mallard. It is true that they visit the estuary and tidal beaches in hard weather when inland waters are frozen, but they soon come back. In 1985 a rotten tree snapped off and fell into the river at the top of our beat on the Dart. It left behind a fat stump 4 or 5 ft high covered with ivy, which no doubt killed the tree in the first place. The top, or crown, of the stump was filled with chips of rotten wood and there, hidden by trails of ivy, a mallard duck laid 14 eggs. We avoided her whilst salmon spinning and in due course she led off 11 ducklings. Three eggs were addled, but a crow or magpie ate them, for within two days just the broken shells remained.

Dropping the rod point when a salmon jumps

29 April 1972. Dart. Two weeks no rain, then about eight hours' rain. Fish taken 12 lb. No. 4 Thunder & Lightning. 11.00 am. This fish risen and pricked half an hour earlier. Rising water. The salmon jumped seven times, hit far bank, took 15 minutes to land.

The above incident provides a wealth of information. The fact that the salmon jumped seven times but was not lost must say something for dropping the rod point whilst the fish is airborne. If one follows this course salmon, and particularly grilse, will still be lost, but not so high a percentage of the total as would come unstuck from a tight line. Why drop the point and thus slacken the line? Look at it this way: swing your arm underwater whilst swimming, and in the air whilst walking. The former movement is slow, being hampered by the water; the latter, in the air, can be fast and jerky. A leader tight to a salmon twisting in the air puts a sharp shock pull on the hook hold which may come away, particularly if the fish falls back on the leader. Movements under the surface are not so abrupt. If the line is loose there is a reduced drag on the hook, unless the jump is at a distance at the end of much drowned line. It is the jump at close quarters where the giving of slack confers most risk reduction on the angler. Of course, the rod must be raised as soon as the salmon is once more submerged, and what a relief it is when the line again comes up tight.

Warning that a jump is imminent is given not more than two seconds before the leap by a violent underwater acceleration of the fish – that is so with two- or three-sea-winter fish. The athletic grilse can hop up at any moment and not much can be done to save a poor hook hold. No wonder the River Teign estuary netsmen call them 'hoppers'.

Look back again at the diary entry: 'This fish risen and pricked an hour earlier.' Fishing with Frazer, head keeper on Darnaway on the Findhorn in the early fifties I had a pull from a salmon. The fish came up from the bottom and took a pluck at one of Frazer's home-tied Findhorn Terrors. These early spring lures were 2 or 3 in. long, with several hooks one behind the other, and must have taken him ages to make. Anyway, this fish gave me a pull. 'Did you prick him?' asked Alec. I nodded. 'He'll no come agin.' And he didn't! Even so, fish do come again at times if pricked, although the interval between each take may be lengthy. Not only was this salmon pricked but he jumped in surprise and shock. This often happens when a fish has pulled and gone. My advice, for what it is worth, is to sit down and wait a while before having another go. This I did, and all the time the water was rising, giving the fish the chance to move on up the river.

Do salmon take on a rising water? Yes, but they're harder to catch than when the fall commences – with one or two exceptions! A productive 10 or 20 minutes at the start of a spate will often be experienced, as the first signs arrive of the water bulge coming down the valley. A group of us were eating lunch in the rain one day, sitting on the edge of the river bed with the lunch basket on the dried out gravel. Suddenly the basket and our boots were awash. We jumped up, started fishing and took a salmon within 15 minutes.

The second opportunity on a rising water is to go to the wide tail of a pool above a stickle, or just above a weir where running salmon, having struggled up, pause for breath and sometimes take. You might just as well stop there, watch and await your chance rather than pursuing fish running up the pools.

CHAPTER 3
MAY

The first two weeks of the month are by no means the best of the chalk river dry fly season, of which May Day is usually 'opening day'. Hatches of natural fly may be inhibited by cold winds and rain, although the iron blue, a brave little fly, likes wet days and will be seen in the roughest weather. There is a promise made by leaf-bursting trees, and all the nesting birds of good warm spells in the third and fourth weeks. By the final days of the month on some rivers the mayfly has arrived, and with it newly hatched ducklings, scuttling across the river to take your artificial fly. Ducklings know a worthwhile fly when they see one, and so do the trout after they have had a day or two in which to grow used to the size of this up-winged, three-tailed floating meal.

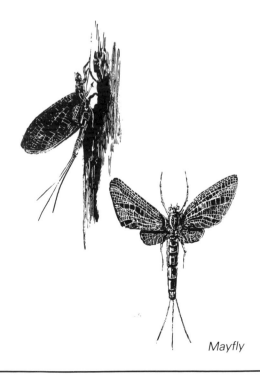

Mayfly

In the first week of the month, or even in late April, there are hatches of hawthorn flies. These are black, land-based, and may be seen in groups rising and falling in flight over warm bushes and meadows; you can identify them by their flat wings and two long, trailing hind legs. Fortunately, the hawthorn fly is often blown onto the water, where it attracts the attention of trout, but more of this later.

On the stocked still waters, reservoirs, lochs and lakes, anglers change from large lures fished deep on sinking lines to the floating line and smaller traditional wet flies. The dry fly, particularly the Black Gnat, brings a reward in the final ten days, or earlier if there is a mild spell. Swifts are about by now, flying fast down wind over the wide water expanse and then turning to move up once more, slowly, whilst scooping flies out of the sky. Swifts have tiny beaks, but their mouths are as wide as their heads. The trout is similar; he has a wide mouth, and like the swift, is capable of taking small items of food at speed.

13 *Stocking trout at Tamar Lake*

Rewarding dry fly fishing on the moorland streams may come in the third week; particularly if a warm shower and mild wind come out of the south or west. These rough bouldered rivers, unkind in a cold breeze, will not readily yield a poacher's pocketful of trout until the warmth of June.

Sea trout have not greatly increased their April rate of entry to the river. In other words, they are still few and far between, but heavier than the July fish.

May is a lovely month for the salmon. Floating fly lines, smaller flies, the surging visible rise and all the fish are still clean and fresh. May is great for quality salmon, and almost all are large, for, as yet, there are no grilse. There are 10-, 15-, 18-pounders and even more; you never know the generosity of the river until you see the first visible underwater turn of a tiring fish or one leaping out of the water.

The dry fly outfit

In Chapter 2 on early season rainbow trout fishing I stressed the necessity of long casting when covering extensive still waters. For this a stiff rod helps, and is considered essential by many. Wet flies and lures are fished below the water surface where a strong leader with a point of 0.009 in. may be used. It is all quite different in upstream dry fly fishing, which may be the only method allowed on many chalk streams, with perhaps the additional use of an upstream nymph after 1 July. Distance casting is no longer important – you may walk up the bank to come within range of a rising trout. What is important is delicacy, and that requires light, well balanced tackle.

14 *A small brown trout hooked on upstream dry fly. River Lyd*

15 *Fishing from a boat at Fernworthy*

Look first at the fly: this must have a light hook or it will sink the fly. Then the leader: this will be fished on the surface film where it will be more visible than the sub-surface wet fly leader. So, your dry fly leader should have no obtrusive knots but be of the knotless tapered variety made to a fine point. Just how fine depends on circumstances: a 5X point of 0.006 in. for the small trout of the moors; 4X of 0.007 in. for Nos 14 and 16 hooked flies on the chalk rivers; 3X of 0.008 in. for a mayfly or fat sedge. Of course, these classifications can only be approximate. One has to bear in mind the size of trout; the presence of weed as a refuge for hooked trout; the 'turnover' of the leader against the wind or when casting a wind resistant mayfly. It is useless to fish a large fly on a fine point – casting will be poor. As with salmon it is wise to use the strongest nylon consistent with hooking the fish; the trout will decide the point diameter for he will refuse it if it is too thick.

In October 1987 I was fishing the Test for rainbow trout with Tony Allen; I tied a used 5X leader to my line. This leader was 6 or 7 in. shorter than the orginal 9 ft and thus, being tapered, would have been thicker at the tip than the original classification. 'Do you think this will be all right?', I asked Tony. 'You'll soon know if it isn't – they just won't take,' he replied. Take they did: grayling, rainbows and browns. We returned these after removing the fly with a tweak of the artery forceps.

When your fine terminal tackle is prepared it must be matched by a rod which will bend to accommodate the stress and absorb the shocks of hooking and playing trout. A rod of easy action between 8ft 6in. and 9ft 6in. in length is ideal. Fibreglass, carbon fibre and split cane are all suitable. Carbon is good for efficiency and lightness on the wrist, split cane is the one if you like your rod to have a soul – the artificial fibre rods somehow lack personality.

Avoid white lines – they flash in the sky and scare trout as one false casts over water. Green is a better colour. The rod manufacturer will make a general recommendation on the line weight AFTM rating to suit the rod, but adapt this suggestion to your particular fishing circumstances. Suppose your rod is rated at AFTM No. 6, then that is probably a good, all-round weight for that particular rod. However, if you are consistently casting a long line on a wide river, reduce the weight to a No. 5 line. If narrow streams are your normal hunting sites then the heavier No. 7 will provide an equal weight in the shorter line length that is held outside the rod tip as you cast.

The AFTM rating of a rod is based on the supposition that the average angler false casts 10 yards of fly line outside the rod tip. If you habitually false cast more or less than this, reduce or increase the line weight. As to the reel – go for a size larger than is necessary to accommodate the fly line and backing which

Moorhen on nest

match your rod. A reel of 3¾-in. diameter will recover line more rapidly than one of 3½-in., provided the spool is full. For this reason do not purchase a reel of 3¼ in. even if it will hold the No. 4 or No. 5 line of a short light rod – the trout will not swim more slowly whilst you whirr the tiny handle! Modern carbon fibre reels, such as those produced by British Fly Reels, are so light in weight that little is gained by cutting down the size, and almost no expenditure is saved.

Little need be said on nets, except that you should use one with a metal bowframe. This type enables you to poke about in a weed bed after the trout you are playing – this cannot be done if the net has two arms joined by a cord at the front. Additionally 'Y'-shaped nets, with opening arms, sometimes fail to extend fully when the points of the arms become entangled in the meshes. Many bowframe nets are of bright shining metal – this may scare a tiring trout into a final escape attempt. Paint such frames green or brown with an aerosol spray of car paint.

Without doubt, the best dry fly boxes are made by Wheatley of Walsall in the West Midlands, in business for many years. I still have one from my school days, which is aluminium, now polished to the patina of old silver. Current models have varied little over the intervening years: the transparent lids of each of the ten compartments spring open at the touch of a finger. Ten sections are just right for the range of eight flies suggested later in this chapter, together with a few mayflies, and one spare compartment for damp specimens. Used leaders may be coiled on the fingers, wrapped a few times with the loop end, and stored in the lid of the box against the etha foam with which it is lined.

Mayfly days

5 May 1976. River Test. Broadlands. The Grove Beat. No salmon about, but some good trout moving. 2½-lb brown on a copper nymph, and a lovely wild brown of 3 lb 14 oz on a mayfly in the Boundary Pool.

On the lower Test it is as well to take a trout rod when salmon fishing. If there are few salmon about, as is usual until late June, there may be a chance at a trout. In those days, Grove was still a salmon beat with no trout stocked, except for the occasional rainbow that had escaped from higher up the river. In 1976 I possessed only one trout fly rod, but that weapon was perfection – an 8 ft 6-in. split cane Hardy CC de France. With this I set about the river. There is little alternative to fishing the river if one does not see a trout taking fly or nymph. Try all the likely runs and eddies, and beside the weed beds. A nymph is best if the trout are down and the copper nymph I used was a Tony Allen Pheasant Tail. This nymph has brought me my two largest trout, both of between 7 and 8 lb. All one needs to produce this fish enticer is a No. 12 hook, fine copper wire and eight or ten fibres of good length from the tail of a cock pheasant.

Back to that first trout: he took sharply in open water beside some metal piling shoring up the bank. We had a great and rapid tussle before the netting. Such a trout, for me, would be remarkable if it had not been overshadowed the same day by his brother of 3 lb 14 oz. This portly fellow was rising mid-river lower down, on a bend, to mayfly, which by then were hatching. A large trout taking natural fly is a memorable sight: the black snout which encloses the insect, the rolling back and dorsal fin, the wide tail which slides away. Several times the rod dropped the bucktail mayfly ahead of his position; it drifted over the leviathan; he did not stir. He has gone down; he saw me; that last throw was splashy; he's been 'lined'. All these depressing thoughts flitted, shadow-like, through my mind. Then, when I looked again, the fly had gone. There was nothing there. Just flat river. It's sunk, I thought, and raised the rod, which bent into a fighting arc. He came to the net after frightening me several times on a 4X leader. Perched on a pinnacle of self esteem, I was soon toppled by Tony, who took one in the same place next week of 4 lb 4 oz. He deserved the lead position, having tied the flies for both of us.

Have you been to a river with a magnificent hatch of mayfly and not a trout to feed upon them in sight? Such a river is, or was, the Dorset Stour at Shapwick, between Wimborne and Blandford. Large pike and roach, substantial chub and a few hefty salmon were there, but apparently no trout. There *are* wild trout there, for others have caught monsters of 3 and 4 lb, and set them up for display above their fireplaces, but they are few in number and wily in the extreme. It seemed such a waste to see all those lovely, upright, gossamer-winged mayflies drifting down as I waded upstream – then a mayfly was sucked down, under a bush. He took me first chuck and went hell bent for the bush roots from which he was soon drawn – a chub. Ah well, life has its disappointments.

The Hampshire Avon is 'fishable' in Wiltshire at Netheravon; it runs down through Amesbury and Salisbury in the same county, crosses Hampshire, and emerges at Christchurch. A magnificent river holding roach, chub, pike, barbel, grayling, salmon and trout. For some seasons in the seventies I had a rod at Lake, between Great Durnford and Amesbury, and there they had a mayfly hatch. There was about a dozen beats, each of perhaps half a mile, and some better than others. The method of beat allotment between the rods was simple: first come, first served. At the fishing hut was a board with numbered hooks, on each of which hung a tally; if No. 6 tally was there, or Nos 5 or 11, as you wished, you took the tally on arrival and hung it up again on departure to show that the beat was free.

One day I took my uncle in return for a day on his water at the salmon of the Welsh Dee. It was mayfly time, and at 10.30 or 11.00 am the insects came up in hundreds. 'It's magic,' he exclaimed, 'One moment there's nothing there and then a fly appears.' I explained the life cycle to him to show him it wasn't so miraculous. The underwater nymph swimming to the water surface, followed by the splitting of the nymphal shuck and the emergence of the dun; the later transformation of the dun to the spinner; mating; egg laying; and then death.

The two or three weeks of the mayfly is a satisfactory time. Here is a fly that everyone can see, regardless of failing eyesight, and tie on. Heavier nylon leaders of 2X or 3X may be used, and should be, for large trout, which feed on the bottom and as cannibals are often on the prowl. Don't expect too much, mayfly fishing is not as simple as all that – 'duffers' fortnight' may raise unfulfilled expectations. For the first two or three days of the hatch the trout are wary of so large an insect; then they start to feed. This is fine unless the hatch is so prolific that there is no reason for them to accept your artificial fly. Then the hooking of the risen trout: it is easy to pull the fly out of his mouth, particularly if your fly is tied with stiff bucktail wings, which protect the hook. Flies made of bucktail are good because they last a long time and float; feather flies, however, gather water and then sink, but are better at taking hold when unused and freshly waterproofed. Personally, I tied a new fly on after each fish, putting the used ones back in a tin to be dried and fluffed up at home.

Mid-May dry fly days

14 May 1987. River Kennet. Hungerford. 1 brown, 3 rainbows. Total 5 lb 1 oz. Best 1 lb 8 oz. Grey Wulff and a bedraggled mayfly. 2 each to Bill and myself.

At the time of this expedition Bill was well into his eighties, and he used the 'bedraggled mayfly'. He needed a fly that was large enough to be seen on the water and one with a good-sized eye to the hook so he could easily attach the fly to the leader. I was using the Grey Wulff, a No. 12, simply because rainbow trout like them. Grey Wulff, Wickham's Fancy, Hare's Ear are all general imitations which rely on good presentation by the angler (no splashy casts) and the dimples (like tiny insect feet) of fine cock hackles pressing on the surface. Some anglers are insect experts, recognizing all the different species as they drift down river, even the tinies. A general understanding of entomology adds to the enjoyment of the day, but one wonders whether the trout, particularly stocked trout of recent entry, know or care about which fly you use. As the warden of one fishery said to me, 'Use something large. These trout don't know the difference between a sedge fly and a loaf of bread: they won't have time to find out either!' This extreme statement enclosed a grain of truth.

General imitations have their place, a favoured place in most fly boxes. You won't lose much by just keeping the following selection: Pheasant Tail Nymph, Wickham's Fancy, Black Gnat, Hawthorn, Kite's Imperial and a Red Sedge. At mayfly time a bucktail offering or a large Grey Wulff are likely to ensure you take your share. Delicate presentation of the fly, fishing at the right time of day, fine nylon, river knowledge – these are of more importance than exact fly imitation. In support consider the experience of a friend of mine, a retired naval commander, who lives a mile upstream of my house on the river Lyd. He came late in years to use the dry fly, but made up for this by a careful study of the river's entomology – nymph, sedge pupa, duns and spinners. He knew them all – but did the trout? He cleaned his catch with care, examining the stomach contents in a saucer of water. Nymphs of stonefly creepers, caterpillars, a wasp, bee, beetles were all there. Then one day he caught a trout on a small dry fly tied to the finest nylon. The fish had a bulge in the flank, and when he cleaned it out he found a small shrew inside, which, from the rawness of the trout's inside, had clearly used its best endeavours to regain the outside world before suffocation. He gave up imitation and became a convert to the Order of the Grey Wulff, a fly which may be dressed with rabbit's fur.

A Dart afternoon

31 May 1984. Dart. Lara and myself had 6 brownies in afternoon. Wickham's Fancy. Ate them for supper. Photographed 3 young carrion crows in tree nest by the river.

There had been a warm rain that morning which had coloured the water a trifle, and raised the river an inch or two. We were at the fishing for about three hours at tea time and each moment was enjoyable. Trout were rising everywhere. Lara used an 8-ft resin impregnated split cane rod whilst I used a carbon at 8 ft 6 in. The leaders were 5X and the fly was dressed on a No. 12 hook. We took no nets, relying on beaching the trout on a gravel bank, or stranding him on a rock mid-river. In these boulder-strewn rivers the best places are the small deep holes, no bigger than 4 yd across, between the rocks. Drag is a problem in these places, but the trout has to make up his mind at once before the current rushes the fly downstream out of his window. He just has time to grab. Short upstream casts, landing the line on a boulder to stop the water taking hold, allowing just the leader and fly to touch the water on the other side – these tactics, with a rapid lift-off after a 2-yd drift, are the answer to fishing the rapid moorland streams. Those trout were beautiful with red spots, golden flanks and white on the leading edges of the anal and pelvic fins. There is nothing like a wild brown trout cooked soon after it has been caught, particularly if it is eaten as an entrée to a grouse shot in the afternoon, both cooked on an open fire of wood and heather roots. For such a feast you would have to journey to Wales or Scotland.

The crow's nest, decorated with red bailer string by the parents, overhung the river in a stunted mountain ash. I climbed the tree, at which disturbance the young birds opened their mouths in supplication for food. The photograph shows yellow-rimmed gaping beaks, red throats and the dark blue bulges of unopened eyes. The parent birds skulked the while in a windswept beech tree several hundred yards away on a hill.

Colliford Lake

29 May 1987. Colliford. Bodmin Moor. Five brown trout, all 10–12 oz. Chrissie caught 2, Martin 2, myself 1. Black Gnat, Hawthorn and Black & Peacock Spider used. First trout to them both.

Colliford is a vast reservoir, natural looking as a lake, and covering 900 acres of former rough grazing. So large an area is unsuitable for stocking as a put and take fishery – the trout would be lost. In consequence, South West Water have followed a policy of introducing annually many thousands of fingerling brown trout. These have grown in the wild conditions since the dam was completed in 1983, and some have reached a large size. The heaviest we took in 1987 was 1 lb 8 oz, on a No. 18 Black Gnat, but many larger trout have been recorded in the fishing hut.

On 29 May we arrived at lunch time in a warm drizzle. Whilst eating our sandwiches a hatch of midges started: the pupae could be clearly seen splitting their cases on the water, and this small fly then struggled free. I tied a No. 18 Black Gnat to a 5X leader, waterproofed the fly with the late Richard Walker's Supafloat, and cast out my offering. A brown trout at once broke through the oily calm water surface and departed with my fly, to be stopped, played and netted. Chrissie and Martin had not fished before this day and took their trout on a Hawthorn, which, to them, was more visible at the limit of their casting range. Later the wind blew up, the insect hatch ceased, and they changed to wet fly, the Black & Peacock, with success. If you wish to fish a small dry fly on an extensive water where the trout are not close to a steep bank, then you must wade. It is not a matter of being unable to cast sufficiently far, but of the distance at which you are able to see your fly and thus be able to raise the rod when the trout takes.

The hawthorn fly

12 May 1982. Tamar Lake. A warm day, south east wind. A good rise to black midges and a few hawthorn. Bill caught 6 trout, Bob Turner-Cain had 2, myself 3. Total 4 browns, 7 rainbows. 10 lb exactly. All caught on black flies.

May can be kind in a southerly wind. These trout were all taken on floating lines with dry Hawthorn or wet Black & Peacock spider. Black flies seem to do well in May, whilst later in the season yellow brings success. Bob, a retired general, positioned himself in a well-chosen tactical battle position at a point where gorse bushes reach the waterside. These bushes and the brambles amongst them are the haunt of flying hawthorn at this time of year: Bob did well with the Black & Peacock. Bill fishes with an old 8 ft 6-in. split cane that always takes its share; the Black & Peacock was also his choice. Meanwhile I used the floating fly. I can see them now, those trout, sucking down my Hawthorn, or boiling under the fly. The hawthorn is a member of Diptera and is never at its best on a cold day; it seems to be a fly which enjoys the warmth of sunny days and the reflection of heat rising up from the yellow flowers of gorse. Of course, it also appears in country lanes, above roads and meadows, and the brambles which will bear blackberries in October.

I am sure the trout are at times frightened of this large fly and, like the mayfly, it takes them a day or two to pluck up courage. Some vigorous rises are not takes at all; perhaps the fish make a disturbance underneath the floating fly by nervously turning away at the final moment, or they are trying to sink the fly to inspect it more closely under water.

The hawthorn is such a heavy insect that it will sink in any case, given time, and this may be behind the success of the Black & Peacock Spider. Dress this fly on a No. 12 hook with a generous body of bronze peacock herl. That the body should be plump will be obvious if you catch a natural one and observe the substantial black thorax. Fish this Spider just below the surface, using a floating fly line – it is a very satisfactory experience if done slowly. Do not fish a Black & Peacock fast when hawthorn are about –after all, a drowning natural is only going to drift with the wind in the gentle progress of the top water.

Sea trout in May

In Devon a sea trout is known as a peal, regardless of size; in Scotland a small one is a finnock but a large one is called a sea trout; in Wales they are sewin. Whatever it is called and wherever it is found, the peal is a mysterious fish. Here today, gone tomorrow. A few small ones, on return from the sea, feed in the river, but the majority, of all sizes, have no appetite. Almost all are shy, most being caught at night by stealthy anglers; others, the minority, will put up with waders thumping in the dark and splashy casting, but there aren't many tolerant ones. May is too early in the season for reliable fishing in the dark, for the nights are cold and the peal have not yet arrived in great numbers. But some have ventured up the rivers, the large members of the tribe, and often more than one might imagine. This was sadly brought home to me at the height of the UDN salmon disease, which also affects sea trout, for there were many dead peal of 2, 3 and 4 lb lying on the river bed of my beat on the lower Dart.

*

Large sea trout will be taken whilst salmon fishing by day, usually in high water conditions.

4 May 1977. Dart. 4-lb sea trout. 5.15 pm. No. 1 Hairy Mary. George had a salmon of 9¾ lb. On 6 May we both rose salmon to the fly without result.

This was in the days when I still used single salmon hooks and the Hairy Mary was a favourite fly. The development of my orange-winged Black Dart tube fly, with No. 8 outpoint treble hook, had yet to take place. On this occasion the 4-lb peal took this large salmon fly in a spate and at first I thought he was a salmon. He was very cross at being hooked, and rushed up and down the river with great verve before losing energy. He then began to sulk under a boulder, several feet from the bank, from which I was unable to draw him, he being on one side and myself on the other. With a terrifying leap I landed on top of his refuge from which I was able to bully him and then land him on his rock with the wire-noosed tailer. Thinking back over the years this must be the only peal on which I have used a tailer – all the others being beached or netted. An oil painting of this peal is in our rod room and the dark encircling line may be seen at the tail wrist where the wire had tightened.

24 May 1985. Dart. A record (for us) sea trout of 7 lb to Lara on a 1-in. Black Dart in the neck of a fast pool.

The peal was taken in a spate on a salmon fly, and I described the capture in my earlier book, *Salmon and Sea Trout Fishing.*

5 May 1986. Dart. Tom's Run. A peal of 2 lb 1 oz. 2-in. Yellow Belly minnow. When salmon spinning. Very fresh and silver. Net marked.

The sad thing about this entry is the record that the trout was 'net marked'. This means that there was a dark rash down the flank of the peal where scales had been rubbed off by a drift or estuary net. For so small a fish just to squeeze through the mesh bunt does not say much for the chances of anything larger.

Leaders for wet flies and lures

You can make the best and cheapest wet fly leader yourself. Take one yard of 20-lb nylon and tie a Blood Bight Loop at one end; join the other end of this section with a Blood Knot to 1 yd of 13 lb; repeat with a point section of 6 or 7 lb. Unlike a floating leader, the junction knots will go unremarked by the trout when sub-surface. The point section may seem a trifle over-powerful, but no nylon is too strong unless it is too visible.

Such a leader may be used with wet fly and lure hook sizes ranging from No. 6 to No. 12 and is my standard for still water trout but for night-time sea trout fishing I like an 8-lb point. Don't forget that a wind knot in the point section of a leader reduces the breaking strain by about 50 per cent; even then, if you hook a 7- or 8-lb trout, you have a good chance of landing your fish.

Be sure to make the leader sink at once when you commence fishing by wiping it with 'sink mix'. Make your own sinking compound by sprinkling Fuller's Earth (available from chemists') and a few drops of washing up liquid on a small piece of wet cloth. The cloth may be stored in the lidded plastic cylinder in which 35 mm films are sold.

16 *Two salmon taken on fly*

Fly tackle for May salmon

I once bartered a salmon caught in early May in 1963. The fish weighed 18 lb, took a No. 6 low water Hairy Mary and was landed on 10-lb FOG camouflage nylon. Cash was not involved in the transaction; instead the innkeeper by the water gave my wife, myself and our two-month-old daughter a free weekend. Impecunious days. The outfit on which this meal ticket was taken was a 12-ft Hardy A.H.E. Wood No. 2 split cane rod, a St John reel of 3⅞-in. diameter and a brown silk line which had to be greased to make it float. I still have the invoice dated 6 February 1958 for the tackle:

Hardy Brothers (Alnwick) Ltd., London Branch, 61 Pall Mall, SW1 6. 2. 58	£	s	d
H5813 12-ft No. 2 AHE Wood rod	22	12	6
St John Reel	5	0	0
No. 6 Corona Line	4	5	0
60 yards, 25-lb Solidae	1	6	0
Purchase Tax	6	16	3
	£39	19	9

The fly on which the salmon was caught was interesting: it came from Gray's of Inverness. The long fine-wired shank of the hook and the lightness of the nylon are enough to make one shudder in a river well endowed with rocks and boulders. Think also of the heavy salmon and know as well that the river was in spate. What can he have been up to? Well, it was just inexperience. Today the nylon would be 15 lb – an untapered 9-ft length straight off the spool in my pocket. The fly? Most probably a 1-in. or 1¼-in. Black Dart or a 1-in. Copper Dart with a No. 8 Partridge X3 outpoint treble.

After 25 years, many salmon and much casting, the Wood rod had suffered enough, become soft in action and had to be replaced by carbon fibre. The St John reel is still going strong in spring with a fast sinking AFTM No. 8 Wet Cel 2 on the spool, supplemented by a wide spooled 3¾ in. Perfect for the floater. This floating line is an Air Cel, plastic coated, which replaces the silk line of yesterday. My telescopic gaff with a cork grip broke up after hitting the salmon of several seasons on the head and, as the gaff is no longer acceptable to me, I now carry a Gye net by a peal sling on my back. Those are the bare bones of a May salmon fly outfit. It is a simple sport, floating line salmon fly fishing, easier in execution than deceiving trout, but relying to a greater extent upon detailed knowledge of the river and a feeling for the water and weather. This feeling develops with the passing of the seasons and is often peculiar to one river. As June arrives and then July you may decide to use smaller flies and slightly lighter nylon, but for the moment look at May when there are large fish and often plenty of cool water in the river.

17 *About to net a salmon in Carradon Ford on Dart. 10 lb* (2 May 1985)

18 Playing the fish at the top of Abbot's Mead. 9 lb (2 May 1985)

A mixed salmon day

2 May 1985. Dart. Noon. Top of Carradon Ford 10 lb, myself. 1-in. Black Dart. 3 pm Top of Abbot's Mead. Brian. 2-in. Blue & Silver Devon minnow. 9 lb. Both very fresh salmon in fine condition.

The year 1985 was a season with a fine spring run. Approximately 45 salmon were taken on the river by early May, of which we had six on our beat. Their weights were 19 lb, 16 lb, 14 lb, 10 lb, 9 lb and 8 lb. On 2 May we took two of these, as the diary records. On that day three men were in my salmon class; we arrived at the river at 11.00 am to find the water at a medium height. Without tackling up, I talked to them, handing over information on salmon and sea trout lies, a discourse which lasted 10 or 15 minutes with my back to the river. We were interrupted by the sound of a splash, not too distinct, behind me – rather weak, I thought, to be a salmon, but one of the men said it was a salmon and pointed out the place. He had seen one leap before, in Scotland.

Running the line through the rings of a 12 ft 6-in. fly rod I put the question to them. Which fly? Large or small? How about colour? They picked out of my box a hair-winged double-hooked Thunder & Lightning, a fly which has a dash of yellow, red and black with jungle cock cheeks to add excitement; and a No. 6 of modest size to match the moderate flow of clear warm water. Keeping low and well upstream of the lie the fly shot out and swam over the fish which rose with startling speed – but did not take. I backed off to rejoin the bankside group. 'Give him ten minutes rest and then an orange-winged 1-in. Black Dart tube fly.' We ate apples; someone smoked a cigarette. He took the Black Dart with a wallop, and off we went downstream, wading thigh deep to work around some trees. After heart stopping antics on his part under the bushes on the far bank he tired, wallowed, and was netted in mid-river. Dave French, the river bailiff, arrived as we knocked the fish on the head and cut out the deeply embedded Partridge treble. 'A grand fly, the Black Dart, but the Copper Dart is even better.' Dave only uses the Copper Dart and I dress the flies for him. In fact this dedication to one fly is no bad thing as it saves dithering about with the contents of the fly box. Such simplicity is possible on the Dart for we only fish in spate conditions, from May onwards to the end of the season, and a substantial fly is required. Faith in one's fly is half the battle, for your offering will spend more time in the water if you desist from changes.

After lunch Brian spun the top of Abbot's Mead with a plastic bodied 2-in. Blue & Silver Devon minnow. Sean was with me 100 or 200 yd down the pool when Brian called faintly from the top. Running to him with advice we all fought a brisk battle down the pool, for the fish had decided to go back to the sea. Trees were negotiated, passing the rod from hand to hand, and the line cleared from the rocks which form the sides of the deep mid-river channel of that pool. He came out in the end, half way down, a bright 9-pounder.

25 May

For three consecutive years in the 1960s salmon fell to my fly on this day. It was all a matter of luck that the water was right and the fish were there. In the 1950s it was the Grand National for three years on the trot! On the river one would be unlikely to do so well today for the spring run is not what it was – the dominant fish are the grilse in many areas. Grilse do not arrive in any remarkable numbers until June, July and onwards. But here, for the record, is what happened.

25 May 1965. Dart. 2.30 pm 15 lb, 3.30 pm 9 lb, 5.30 pm 7½ lb. This day was remarkable. Fished all morning with no sign of a salmon; it was raining all the time. Had lunch. Rain ceased and these fish were all caught on the same No. 6 Low water Hairy Mary. Water medium/low.

There come days to all of us when the weather changes for the better, the atmospheric pressure lifts, and fish come on the take. This was one of those days. The nine-pounder nearly escaped me by running out of the pool tail, but I was able to follow by climbing a tree to take the rod around the trunk and through the branches. Whilst stuck in the tree limbs I called to walking passers by on the road for help, but none came. 'There be a nut case stuck in a tree back there. Shoutin' 'is aid off ee be. Best to let un be m'dear. Ee be a furriner from up-country.' I could just hear them, but I had my fish.

25 May 1966. Dart. Water temperature 49° F at 9.00 am. 51° F at 1 pm. Water medium height and coloured after rain. 10.30 am 8 lb. Hairy Mary. 1.30 pm, 9½ lb, No. 2 Thunder & Lightning.

and:

25 May 1967. Dart. Heavy rain previous day and overnight. River running strong but clear 8.00 am. Fished until 3.00 pm, water dropped 6 in. Took fish 11½ lb. No. 6 Thunder & Lightning. Fish went down through lower gap three times at run-off, each time I was able to walk it up. This pool fished at 10.00 am without result before the water had warmed and dropped. 4.00 pm took another of 7½ lb on same fly whilst wading river with fly trailing free downstream.

That final fish was one of the most helpful one could meet. But what is meant by 'walking up'? When a fish makes a dash for the tail of a pool you can often stop him from actually going out by dropping the rod point and removing all pressure. This causes the salmon to swing about and face up the river so that the water may enter his mouth and pass out through his gills; he has to breathe. You will find it takes courage and must be done in good time with several yards of water to spare. Following this action one may again raise the rod to re-establish contact. However, the fish is still at the extreme lower end of the pool and must be brought up-river and away from this dangerous area. This is accomplished by 'walking up'. Having tightened gently on the salmon, point the rod out over the river at right angles to the bank and horizontal then, without reeling, increase the upstream draw until you are able to walk slowly and gently up the river. The salmon will follow in three cases out of four. The essence is in the lack of jerks and vibrations: do not use the reel. Think of this manoeuvre as sliding the streamlined fish through unresisting water which parts before his nose. When you have him up nearer the head of the pool you may raise your rod and move down opposite to his position – this re-positioning will stir him to action owing to the altered direction of the pull, the pressure of water on his flank, and the need to counteract these forces.

A black fly for Fernworthy in May

In 1987 Fernworthy has been stocked regularly with brown trout of 1 lb and over. In 1986 and earlier seasons the stocking was with rainbows. It doesn't seem to matter which fish is put in, they both like black flies early in the season. Later in the year, August and September, a period which the Scots delicately describe as the 'back end', they have a preference for yellow. I will discuss this weakness later.

21 May 1981. Fernworthy. Sally caught 2 rainbows including her first. Mike made a good start with 2, of which 1 was 2 lb, then had to leave for Oxford. Pete had 2 more, myself 5. In all, 12 trout, totalling 15 lb 12 oz. A very good rough day. All on Black Muddler.

and:

21 May 1982. Fernworthy. Bunny and Joanna, Jonathan, Simon and Hugh. A good day with a strong west wind. Most fish caught on the surface on Black Muddlers. We took 5 rainbows and 9 brook trout of 17 lb 2 oz. First trout to Joanna, Jonathan and Hugh.

also:

3 May 1987. Fernworthy. 2 brown trout of 2 lb 15 oz. Best 1 lb 8 oz. Black Pennel. James fished for half a day.

Looking back through the diary, over the years, the Black Muddler, Black & Peacock Spider, Black Chenille and Sweeney Todd are consistently successful in this reservoir. Perhaps it is due to the clarity of the water, but you may have noticed that all these flies, with the exception of the B & P, have black *striped* bodies. So has the Black Dart tube fly for salmon, and the Black Lure which is a favourite sea trout fly. The scientists, who say that striped items attract fish, must be right. In other waters that are not so clear, red, orange and yellow may be more rewarding – and this applies to salmon rivers. Yellow flies and Yellow Belly minnows seem to take salmon better then dark flies in the lowland rivers carrying swirls of mud after rain.

The three May days given above saw us using floating lines. Black flies are also effective when fished deep and not only in May: in a heatwave it pays to take a large lure down to the depth to which trout have descended for coolness. In May all the water is cool and if a cold wind inhibits natural insect activity it is as well to sink the fly.

9 May 1980. Fernworthy. We fished all day in a cold east wind. No surface activity. Phillip (the warden) encouraged us with a visit. Between 3.30 pm and 4.00 pm we had 3 rainbows of 1 lb 3 oz each, and one monster of 5 lb 10 oz on a Black Muddler fished deep by the North burn. The fish only came on for half an hour in the whole day, and we were fishing in the right place at the correct depth.

19 *'Brownie' Hardman with three small ones in her net, and the 5 lb 10 oz rainbow on her index finger. Fernworthy (9 May 1980)*

A Hairy Mary on the Findhorn, by James Stuart

The lines of dark-backed spring fish holding their stations below the falls at the head of the pool had been gone for some weeks, drawn like mercury up the Findhorn's narrow gorges by the increasing temperature of the water. It was May and above us, edged with black serrations of jutting rocks and a tumble of Scots pine, beech and oak, the sky was a narrow blue band, full of sunlight and the promise of warmth. Emma, my friend from Kentucky, shivered: her southern blood a shade thin for the blue-brown shadows of the deep gorges lining this section of the river with their layered walls of sedimentary rock soaring above a base of smooth, glacier-grey granitic boulders, colder than the air we breathed and the peat-dark water gliding by.

We crouched on an outcrop of rock 20 ft from the tail of the pool, which was split by a pink boulder some 12 ft wide and 6 ft high, forming two narrow glides. Above the further glide some 20 ft from where we stood is a magic patch of water where, if there is a fish in the river, one may almost always be found. The rub is that leaning over the water at this point is a rounded extrusion of purplish-blue rock which bars the lie to any fly not fished in the certain manner. 'Threading the needle', was how our old keeper used to describe the process.

Previously, Emma had fished the Spey at Tulchan and the Little Gruinard on the West Coast, the latter coming close to demanding the precision now required. We knew that a good fish had taken up residence in the buttressed lie: we had seen it dimly as, goat-like, we'd clambered down to the pool ten minutes earlier. Emma shivered again: probably at the thought of hooking a fish in so restricted a pool, but also at the challenging task ahead. To thread the eye of this particular needle securely required a short Spey cast that ended up with the last 3 ft of the line draped across the overhang of smooth rock, with enough cast trailing in the water on the far side to allow the fly to waft slowly across the lie before being pulled away to the nearside glide.

From my rocky roost, high above Emma perched on her own granite pinnacle which rose from the water's edge, I could see every move. On the first cast the line missed the overhang and, as the fly scudded off the lie, a dull gleam below signalled the fish's intent. Now for a cast through the needle's eye! The fly was an abused Hairy Mary; its tattiness a virtue by reason of its popularity with several fish. (Besides, I concluded, somewhat meanly, this Hairy Mary was of pensionable age. Should she be broken on the rocks her loss, while mourned, would be timely.)

The line appeared to hover above the rock as the cast floated down beyond the overhang: the needle had been threaded. I swear Emma's hair stood at right angles to her head as for two seconds the fly lazed on the lie. The white of the inside of the fish's mouth showed cleanly as it took the fly then turned with a flash of gold down to its lie. As the line bellied down and out in the current, my friend felt the fish: her fingers locked around the reel. She froze.

A small white bow-wave developed at the point where the line sliced into the water as the fish headed upstream. Twelve feet of carbon shortened to six as the rod bent double, then eased as Emma's arms straightened, the rod all but parallel to the water. One of three things would happen: the hook would pull, the cast would break, Emma would wind up in the river. Unless, that is, her customary sang-froid was restored and soon.

We laugh about it now, but as I slid from my rocky perch, tore the cap from my head, filled it with water which I poured over her head, I saw a beautiful friendship being washed away. Chilly Findhorn water is apparently good for fisherladies from Kentucky as well as lively salmon. The manic grip relaxed. The reel sang merrily and within ten minutes a well-tailed fish lay like a rainbow at our feet. Emma wiped her eyes: Findhorn water or tears, I could not tell. Nor dared I ask. . . .

CHAPTER 4
JUNE

In these four weeks are encapsulated the final days of spring and the first taste and promise of fulfilling summer fishing. The season is not yet sad, as in September, for there are many bountiful weeks ahead; the end is not in sight. We may fish in warm contentment, without hurry.

At the opening of the month many trout rivers will be entering the final phase of the mayfly; on others, the 'duffer's fortnight', as the mellow period of the hatch is called, will be about to start. Dry fly takes precedence on the trout still waters for those who enjoy using it. In the last half of June the first of the grilse arrive in our rivers and the sea trout start to invade the valleys. June is a fishing month of the highest quality, but it exacts of us a quality performance. Sea trout are there, but we must find them in the dark. Grilse are present, but few in number and only to be caught on fishing days which coincide with those short spells

Chinese water deer

when the river is in ply. Trout are 'on the fin', but many are well educated, having taken a look at us in May. And the salmon? Large salmon of two or three sea-winters still outnumber their younger brothers, the one-sea-winter grilse.

Ducklings still scuttle after mayflies on the river top, and the cuckoo becomes monotonous. Young rabbits on the lawn, pigeon squabs on draughty nesting platforms in the blackthorn bushes, the bluebell, the first green uncurling thrust of the bracken on the hill. Orange Tip butterflies, and sedge flies at the waterside. June is all of these for those who look – the listeners who breathe the virgin scent of dawn and leave their trail of footsteps in the early morning dew.

Backing up the fly for salmon

In June 1959, five salmon came my way in six days' fishing whilst staying at Kilphedir on the Helmsdale. I clearly remember one of these fish, but not the name of the pool. Anyway, it was long, wide and with a main current down the centre which one fished from a high right bank. One or two fish were showing but all were covered from the neck to the run off without responding to the fly, a low water Hairy Mary. 'Tie this on, and back it up,' said the gillie, proffering a Lady Caroline. 'Back it up. How do I do that?' He told me, showed me, and sealed the fate in those two or three minutes of many future salmon. Starting at the run-off cast almost square across the pool, take two backward steps upstream whilst retrieving line at the same time. The result of this is that the fly crosses the river in a fast curve, you put your foot in a rabbit hole, and the gillie picks you up! However, if you are fit, sober, and well balanced this need not be the order of progress. Backing up the pool you work towards the top and sooner or later, if luck is with you, there will be a boil of water and the rod will buck and jump in your hands. The take usually occurs after the fly has crossed the main stream and is starting to straighten downstream of your position, just as the fly whips around in the final curve. Salmon caught whilst backing up are usually well hooked for they engulf the fly wide-mouthed at speed, closing their jaws as they turn down. No response is required of the angler; it is all too fast for that, and in any case he is already doing his bit by walking backwards.

The common way of employing this method is to fish down the pool, casting down and across and then, when the tail has been reached, to back up. But sometimes it is better not to fish down at all, but to begin at the tail of the pool and start by backing up. To illustrate these suggestions consider the following:

27 June 1982. An extraordinary day. Started at 8.00 am in Iron Bars. At 8.20 am took 9-lb salmon in middle stickle on 1¼-in. Black Dart. Took 8 minutes to land. Fished down to Splay Pool. On the way back, in various pools, most of which I had fished on the way down river, I rose 8 salmon. Most of these fish did not touch the fly, but 3 nipped it and came off almost at once. Finished at 1.10 pm.

This day was a failure and provoked much thought. Fishing had been in the conventional manner, and even on the way back had still been 'down and across' casting, starting at the head of the pool. Perhaps the size of fly was wrong, but this is doubtful, for larger and smaller ones would certainly have been tried. Two years later the same situation arose. Again the start was at 8.00 am. Again the casting was 'down and across'; by lunchtime four fish had risen to pass by the orange fly at close quarters and return to their lies. It was almost possible to hear them remark to each other: 'Just another of those deceitful creations'. I sat down, had lunch of sandwiches and a tin of beer, then set about the downfall of these fish. Two salmon were risen, hooked and landed. Both were cock fish of 10 lb, and the fly a 1¼-in. Black Dart. They fell to the backed up fly, but not after the pool had been fished down first. There is much to be said for *starting* at the tail of the pool: this increases the surprise element which is, to my mind, one of the most telling factors in taking salmon. When one progresses down a pool the salmon sees the fly so many times, as it comes closer, that he must be sick of the sight of it by the time his lie is reached. He is much more likely to take the fly on impulse the first or second time he sees it if these arrivals *are in his taking area.* Backed up flies arrive suddenly, moving fast – he must take or lose the chance.

One may carry this practice further, with notable success, by ignoring the whole pool with the exception of the two or three yards that you know, from experience, are likely to hold a salmon. Go to these places first; cover the vital area with your initial cast. The resident torpid salmon will be startled, and the chances are he will come up with a rush and go down hooked. There is one matter to be closely watched – concealment. A salmon can see nothing below a 12° angle above the water surface. If you are casting downstream, long and far off, you are likely to be within this angle and out of sight. This is not the case in backing up when you may be opposite the lie and substantially above the fish in height. Concealment and stealth are therefore important: keep back from the bank; fish from behind a screen of low bushes; use a tree as background to cut out silhouette.

In 1984 my youngest daughter, Lara, took her first salmon on a 1¼-in. Black Dart whilst backing up. The fish weighed 10½ lb. I had already fished over the water in the downstream method, for we were sharing a rod whilst the other carried a camera. The pool was not wide but she cast at right angles over to the far bank and, as the fly curved across the river at speed, this salmon surged up from the bottom to take with determination. A fish of that weight as a 'first' on a fly rod is an exciting introduction, which is why we took no photographs of the battle, for the netsman was too busy.

Hooking salmon on the dangle

1 June 1983. The Slide. 8½ lb. 1-in. Black Dart.

The Slide is a narrow, smoothly flowing run about 2 yd wide and 4 or 5 ft deep. It is only 7 or 8 yd in length, and the salmon lie half way down. Although the flow is smooth, it is also fast and there is little room for a salmon to take and turn with the fly. Instead they come up, take, and then sink back from sight. The fisherman needs to see what is happening when he casts, which can only be done standing on a rock a yard out from the bank and directly upstream of the salmon lie.

As you can see, if my description is clear, the fly is on the dangle all the time. It is a place which only holds a fish in warm water and, as the current prevents the fly from being held down, the salmon has to come up. When he does, you view, not the salmon, but a wide-open white-rimmed mouth. What will you do? Raise the rod? I hope not. All you see is the white-lipped orifice, and whilst you see that you must do nothing or you will just draw the fly out of his mouth. When the mouth has closed, and you are hard put to see the fish, is the time to raise the rod. The chances are that the fish is then drifting back to his lie without turning, water pressing on his back, head down. If you tighten at this moment the treble will probably dig into the cavity under his snout. You willl not be able to land a salmon in such a place. To land him he must be persuaded up or drawn down to wider quieter waters. There was a fish I remember in the dangle position on a day which brought three salmon. He was not one of them. He rose in the morning, he rose after lunch, and he came up for his tea, but he had dreadful manners and never ate with his mouth shut. There was no point in raising the rod for he always sank away with his jaws open and never gave a touch or pull. He had me hopping mad on the rock, where I was fishing for him with the line 'on the droop'. In the end, in disgust, I dropped the rod point, the fly was washed down beyond his playground, and a second salmon helped himself.

'On the droop' means that one fishes with the rod held high, and thus the line curves slackly down to the river surface. The stance is particularly helpful in places such as The Slide, for as the salmon sinks away, closing his mouth, he straightens the droop and then the angler tightens.

There is another lie which is fished on the dangle and in this place the run is a trifle wider, giving the salmon just enough room to turn. The trouble with this place is that the salmon takes just two yards below your rod point, in full view. If I am missing one day, look for me there – the autopsy will reveal a heart attack. The way to hook these fish is to draw the correct length of line from the reel then, before you cast, pull off 2 more yards, hold these in your fingers and mutter to yourself, 'if he comes up I will let go and do nothing'. You cast, up he comes, you let go the 2 yards whilst the flank is visible, away he goes, you raise the rod to tighten the line and scamper off downstream to reach the netting place before him.

The sedge fly season

Look into the small pools and backwaters of a moorland stream in June and there, on the bottom, will be dozens, sometimes hundreds, of small cylindrical cases. Made of sand, pieces of old leaf or other vegetable matter, they appear to be motionless. Look closely, and at those which appear to be stuck half way up the sides of underwater boulders, and you may detect slight movement. If you pick one up you will see that one end is open and the other sealed. Let the cylinder rest motionless on someone's hand and a head will peer out of the open end, legs will follow the head and the sedge larva will take a walk across the palm. In time, the larva will seal up the open end and change to a sedge fly inside – in the same manner as chrysalizing butterflies and moths. To hatch, the fly opens up the end once more, crawls to the surface, leaves the protecting home, dries its wings and flies away. The sedge fly season starts in earnest in June. By September you will be hard put to find an occupied underwater case, for the season will be almost over.

There are red, grey, brown, black and yellow sedges. For myself, it has proved sufficient to carry in the fly box a winged or hackled Red Sedge. On some waters a better choice would be the Caperer. This fly is aptly named owing to the habit of the female of skittering up and down over the water surface in the evening as she lays her eggs. Instructions for dressing the Caperer may be found in many books, but the outstanding features are the dark hackles and the band of yellow-dyed swan feather which forms a circle in the centre of the body.

1971. River Allen. Dorset. In June I caught a brownie of 1 lb 11 oz on a Caperer at dusk just above the lake outflow.

This took place where the river runs through the Crichel Estate. The catch is worthy of a mention because the trout was wild, had been noted for two or three evenings, and eventually fell to this fly in a sheltered area under trees and bushes, and between reed beds.

26 June 1981. Fernworthy. Sedges and a late hatch of hawthorn fly. John, 2 rainbows; Bryan, a limit of 5; myself, 3. We fished dry Hawthorn and Red Sedge. Total about 10 lb.

The end of June is late for the hawthorn fly, but then everything is late on this water which is chilly in the first half of the season, being 1,050 ft above sea level. The rhododendrons behind the dam bloom three or four weeks behind those in lower regions, and opening day is one month later than many still waters. Bryan fished from the bank; John and myself shared a boat anchored close to the north shore from which the wind was blowing fly onto the water. We used 4X leaders for these substantial flies and cast just up-wind of those trout which could be seen cruising along, picking off their victims. Bryan took his limit of five in good time, and generous fellow that he is, offered to help me out. The offer was accepted, but even so the boat catch stayed at five.

The occupants of boats on some waters, where professional boatmen are not employed, spend as much time rowing, and shifting about the place as in fishing. Whilst there are quite clearly waters which cannot be fished other than from a boat, my preferred method is to fish from the bank if the trout are within casting range. One may concentrate on the fishing, make less disturbance, and a caster of adequate performance usually beats his waterborne rival.

A mixed June day

28 June 1987. Dart. Salmon 11 lb on 1-in. Copper Dart. 8-oz brown trout on Red Sedge. Salmon hooked by me, played by Giles.

This weekend class of two fathers and sons had gone to the Dart to fish dry fly for trout. Ever hopeful, we took one salmon fly rod with us, there having been a little rain in the previous 48 hours. Perhaps there would be a chance – one is never entirely sure with salmon. We reached the river and started with a discourse on salmon lies and how these alter with the height of the water. We decided that there wouldn't be a salmon in the tail of the pool – that would only be worth trying in high water. Nor in those two lies half way up this trench;

20 *Hooking an 11-lb salmon on a 1-in. Copper Dart tube fly. Dart (28 June 1987)*

21 Handing the rod to Giles, 'Don't let the fish go downstream.

22 Giles takes over

23 *The salmon tries to run downriver, is checked and becomes cross*

24 *Head first into the net*

25 *The salmon is safe unless I slip*

26 *The catch*

these were suitable only for a medium height water. It was just possible that we might interest a fish in the rough water at the neck. Almost certainly there would be a salmon there, waiting for a week or two for the next spate, but with this low water he probably wouldn't be interested.

We selected the smallest of the three sizes of tube fly in the box, a 1-in. Copper Dart with No. 8 Partridge X3 treble hook. Out came the spool of 15-lb nylon, at the end of which we tied a Blood Bight Loop for the fly line attachment; we cut off 9 ft, threaded the tube and tied on the hook with a Tucked Half Blood. The hook eye was then drawn up into the socket at the tail of the tube where the polythene held it in line. The four spectators stood back from the bank whilst the fly was cast into the neck from a concealed low down stance upstream. He came up, rivetting our gaze. We had all been a little bored by poor trout catches in the previous two days. Nothing had been expected. This salmon broke the surface – and alerted us all. The second cast he took,

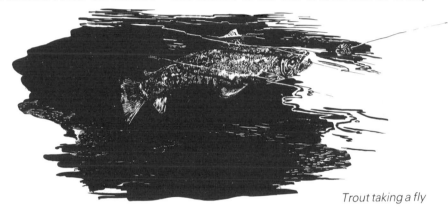

Trout taking a fly

turned down out of sight and was hooked by the rising rod which I placed in Giles's eager but inexperienced hands. 'So far as you can keep opposite to him, hold the rod tip high and the line "up and down"; this will stop the fish taking a turn around a rock. If he jumps lower your rod point. If he rushes for the pool tail, slack off. Don't hang on tight.' Brave Giles – the responsibility was his. We netted the fish as it should be done –head first.

After lunch we set about the trout with 8 ft 6-in. or 9-ft rods of gentle action, 5X leaders, Kite's Imperial, Wickham's Fancy and Red Sedge – casting upstream. 'The great thing about dry fly is to avoid drag. The fly must drift down at the same speed as the current, whilst you gather in the line at the speed of drift with your free hand. There are advantages: you are below the level of the trout as the river runs downhill and, if careful, will be out of sight; when you have a rise and strike to set the hook the chances are that the fly will take hold in the scissors of his jaws.' I chatted away before casting up under some bushes where this half-pound brown obliged. Half-a-pound! He's baby snatching. Well, not really. You see the trout in acid moorland rivers are small. Half-a-pound is a trout of note. A fish of strength, verve and guile who almost escaped amongst the rocks.

Trapping pike

On a dairy farm, where the main crop may be grass, a weed is a plant in the wrong place in the sward. The weed itself may not be unwanted, in fact it probably has a number of desirable characteristics: an attractive flower, resistance to treading by cattle, the provision of minerals, and the ability to withstand drought and stay green. But if grass is the crop, and milk or meat the product, a weed is a plant out of place.

The same applies to pike, which have been called the coarse fisher's salmon. On many clear, stark, frosty days in January and February, a few hours spent spinning for pike with your salmon tackle is a delightful escape from the house, when the eyes and mind stretch themselves away from the restricting warmth of the fireside. Such a day is a joy: the river weeds have been killed back by the frost, the water is clear, the copper spoon wobbles and flashes. Then, with all the suddenness of a rising salmon, a pike, of savage size, charges out of the roots of the riverside trees and takes the spoon. Such a happening is grand, an event to which one may look forward.

As a boy I remember not quite so satisfactory a moment as a dace, hooked after much inexpert and persistent casting of a Black Gnat, was nobbled by a pike as it was played back to my eager reaching hands. Worse, there is the possibility of the loss of a trout in the same manner on a chalk stream. To lose a

27 A pike trap. The wide mouth in the front is at the downstream end when placed in the river

hooked trout to a pike is not a common experience. This is not because there aren't many trout or pike in a well stocked river. Pike always seem to be present in alkaline chalk rivers – but these fish are cunning. They also do not need to take more than one or two trout a week, but each trout may be worth a guinea. All hands are thus against them. They are a fish out of place. Fortunately, a pike is not a difficult fish to trap, and this may be accomplished without a great deal of effort. The pike trap works on the principle of the lobster pot, but without the bait, and the unspillable ink wells of the classrooms of 40 years ago: once inside the fish cannot find his way out.

There is such a trap at Bossington. The cage is placed in a tributary of the river, a side stream or ditch, into which pike will swim in spring to spawn. The wide mouth faces downstream, blocking as much of the channel as possible; the pike enters, goes through the lobster pot orifice and is trapped. There he stays until the cage is visited, and he may be removed through one of the wire netting side doors. The fish might be killed, or transferred to a lake where it is not out of place – a coarse fishing scene. In a smaller trout river the trap may be placed in the main run, preferably between two weed beds which restrict the river to a narrow channel in that place. The pike, going about his normal business, swims into the cage in his progression from one pool to the next. Such a trap ought to be visited each day. On the river Allen in Dorset, in summer, we had such a system and three of us, fishers who had rods on the river, attended the trap on a rota basis. The rota went wrong on one occasion and no inspection was made for ten days. I was the first to visit after this interval. A pike had died inside, providing an unexpected windfall feast for the river crayfish, of which there were a bucketful inside the wire. I released the majority, but took half a dozen in a bucket of water to show the pupils of the local school. We then put them back into the Allen.

Chalk stream weed cutting and silt removal

Silt deposition and unwanted weeds are the bane of a river keeper's life, and if not kept under control, they can ruin a river in a short period of time. Not all weed is unwanted: a controlled series of weed beds across a river prevents water from running away in summer and is a haven of fly life.

Weed growth is closely related to silt deposition: the more weed, and thus the slower the water flow, the greater will be the build-up of silt. Silt is no longer an inert deposition: today the make up is not only mud deposited by natural causes, but includes farming chemicals washed into the river by seasonal rains and, most undesirable of all, the excreta released from the many trout farms which seem to be allowed to spring up wherever water is to be found. Additionally, too much silt delays desirable weed growth, which in turn affects fly life, and also masks the river bed in trout-spawning areas. Weed and silt thus go hand in hand – a little of each is an asset, too much of either and the keeper is in trouble.

28 *The weed cutting boat*

29 *Silt control boom. The far tethering rope is visible below the bank; the near rope is under the weeds in front of the nearest plank*

Traditional methods of controlling river weed were time-consuming and required much physical effort. They were largely carried out by the keeper wielding a scythe and wearing chest waders. This is a hot task in summer and if the man goes in too deep he bobs away downstream! The scythe is still in use, but a faster labour saving method is the power driven weed cutting boat. This operates on the principle of the old-fashioned grass cutter with reciprocating knives between vegetation guiding fingers.

There are set periods on a river for weed cutting in the fishing season. During these spells of activity, much disliked by the angler for the disruption to his sport caused by the drifting flotsam, the river must be kept open to allow free downstream passage to the drifting weed.

The removal of silt is carried out in the winter and must cease at the end of February. A common and tedious way of cleaning the river bed is to stake out sheets of corrugated iron at an angle, thus diverting the current which, speeded up in the restricted gap, will wash away an area of silt. This method is difficult, labour intensive, tedious and not particularly efficient. There is the further disadvantage that, if forgotten and left over-long in one position, an area of bank may be washed out on the other side of the river.

The boom is a much better device which spans almost the complete width of a medium-sized waterway. The boom is kept in position by ropes at each end which are attached to stakes driven into both river banks. The action of the boom clears about 10 yd of the river bed in approximately one hour; it is then moved downstream by slackening the ropes, or re-attaching them to further downstream stakes. The compressed, speeded up water, diverted below the boom, washes away the silt. The illustration of this home-made device shows a system which is not an entirely new idea, but in this improved form, boards are incorporated and extend, like the keel of a boat, towards the river bed, causing extra turbulence.

A River Test afternoon

3 June. Bossington. Tony and myself shared a rod. 4 browns. 6 lb 1 oz. A small midge.

This water, immediately below the Houghton Club near Stockbridge, is looked after by Brian, who is head river keeper. At the time, he was in his second season after some years as under-keeper at Broadlands, lower down the river. Brian deeply hopes that the water should again be the haven of brown trout, with rainbows as a secondary back-up. Grayling, as well as the few rainbows, are welcome to make up a balanced river population.

We fished that afternoon by invitation of one of the season rods, one old split cane rod between the two of us, taking turns at rises, whilst the other watched for a further feeding fish. At first the water surface was flat, uninterrupted by

30 *A brown trout placed in the shade, and marked by crossed rushes on the grass path. River Test (3 June 1987)*

31 *Tony Allen hooking a trout on 1 ½ lb nylon and a No. 20 midge (3 June 1987)*

32 The trout under control . . .

33 and netted . . .

movement, almost dead. We wandered up the bank looking for a trout – and then there was a dimple, a tiny pimple stretching the water skin upwards as a trout took a midge. The insect was too small to be seen. Tony fishes very fine, 1.9-lb Dai-Riki 7X nylon, to which he was introduced by Marty Sherman, Editor of the American magazine *Flyfishing*, who gave him a spool when fishing the upper Test the previous season. To this fine point we tied a midge, a tiny creation of brisk grey/brown hackles, with a Turle knot, on a No. 20 hook. The whole was as gossamer light as a dandelion seed on a spider's thread – and yet only one trout, once hooked, had the better of us. It all seems so easy, so successful and looks so simple when Tony fishes for trout. However, it is not plain sailing, but something satisfying to learn how to master. We had four trout as we progressed up the bank, leaving each in the shady undergrowth, marking the dropping points with a pair of cut, crossed rushes.

It is always the salmon which you lose, the sea trout which has the better of you, and the trout which rises, sips and bulges without taking your fly which you remember. So it was that afternoon with one particular trout which had taken up a position under a bush, one foot out from the bank, in a depth of 6 in. of water. He was impossible. At that depth his vision window could only be 1 ft in diameter, and that 1 ft circle was under the bush whose twigs almost swept the water. Of course he had to be tried – of that there was never any question. Side casting carefully, with the rod horizontal and almost touching the river, I propelled the fly through the 6-in. gap between the water and the hanging twigs. The trout was deceived. He took. After much frothing, splashing and crossness under the bush, the fly came back – a trout to be remembered, but never tasted.

34 *I play a brown trout on Tony's rod . . .*

35 *Keep low – trout fight hard even if they cannot see the angler . . .*

36 *Safely in the net*

The grilse

From the time salmon ova hatch in early spring, through the stages of alevin, fry and parr, two years pass until, as smolts, they leave the river for the sea in April and May. At this stage the smolt weighs about 10 oz and is barely 10 in. in length. The rich feeding provided by the sea lifts his body weight to 4, 5 or 6 lb in 15 to 18 months. Sometimes grilse weigh more if the foraging has been good and an extra month or two has been spent at sea. Then back they come to the rivers of their birth; from June onwards to October, and possibly a little later on some rivers. June sees the start of the grilse run, usually in the final week, but it is only the start, for greater numbers enter, when full water allows, as the season progresses through the summer. On my beat, on the lower Dart, they are scarce this month – a catch is an event. In September, when there is often more and cleaner water, it is a different matter – you may almost rely upon September. In between, in July and August, we are often plagued by low water, with only an occasional spate. Not only is the water from these spates likely to be dirty after dry spells, making fishing unrewarding, but the grilse, frustrated by delay, run upriver quickly. A running fish is hard to catch! The lower down river your beat, the harder your task, because the grilse run rapidly past, only showing when they reach the top third of the river. It seems that salmon and grilse have an alarm clock in their heads. The bell is set for the end of November, by which time, when it goes off, most fish should be on the spawning beds, although on some rivers it may be later. The salmon knows all about this, taking his time or speeding his journey up the river according to the month of entry. Grilse enter in the second half of the season, running a long way and fast on floods which may be few and far between. In consequence they rush through the lower beats and are, therefore, hard to catch.

30 June 1974. Test. Broadlands. Rookery and Beat No. 1. James Stuart came with us. 1.00 pm. 4½-lb grilse on prawn. River going down after a spate. Gave half the fish to James to take back to London.

Lunch in the fishing hut at the bottom of Rookery beat, just by that groyne known as Blackpool Pier, is a meal of prolonged pleasure. That is, if you have a good lunch, suitably beveraged. That day we washed our food down with Gallic wine and the Scottish product. It is difficult to fish with athletic step and remain clear of eye after a lunch in the Rookery Hut. Mind you, that was our host's intention, for whilst we wander about happily in the afternoon he concentrates on the best places and most prolific lies.

James said the grilse we caught was the smallest he had seen, and he is well qualified to comment, having taken many from the Findhorn in Morayshire. It is doubtful if the half he took back to town at the end of the day would have provided a meal for four.

The prawn is not a bait I like to use, but it has a wide range of river conditions in which it may be fished. There are times and places where it is a more productive method than spinning with an artificial minnow or fishing with the fly. You may try a large prawn in the cold March river and a small one in summer. Use the prawn in clear water through which you can see the salmon you intend to catch, and in a clouded river, close to the bottom, when the salmon would be hard put to see a fly close to the surface. It is a versatile bait. There is excitement when fishing by the paternoster method; the weight bumping its way, yard by yard, down towards the lie whilst you feel the line between your fingers, waiting for the twitch of a taking fish. The twitch could be just an eel, but it could be a 20-pounder. Prawning, when you cannot see the bait or quarry, is like a lucky dip. The most exciting moments arise when the salmon is visible, the grey shadow resting on the river bed between flanking beds of weed. At times the mouth of such a fish opens and the white edges are visible. To catch that one you need to wear polaroid glasses and use a long rod and a weight of about 1 oz. The prawn may then be swayed a foot or two in front of his nose, tantalizing him, whilst you await the mouth opening and forward movement of the fish. Some say you should give him time when he has the prawn in his mouth, but it is probably better to strike at once. A salmon is able to mouth a prawn and then blow it out so fast that the angler is unable to react in time.

Upstream Mepps at Broadlands

12 June 1977. Test. Rookery. Just above point of Island Pool. No. 5 upstream Mepps. 9 lb with sea lice.

When the water warms in late spring, and then through the summer and autumn, salmon may be caught by casting a bait straight upstream. Throw the lure as far as you can, allow it to sink a foot on hitting the river surface and then reel back faster than the current. The rapid downriver movement over the heads of the fish stirs the automatic response of a predator, the salmon gives chase – sometimes, but not always, taking the bait. Many times they veer away at the final moment, sheering off under your feet with the flash of a silver- or copper-coloured flank, the colour depending upon the time of year.

It is as well not to have any weight at the line/trace junction; just tie in a ball bearing swivel, for there is no need to sink the bait deeply as salmon will rise up from the river bed. The fixed spool reel with a monofilament line of 18 lb, and a 15-lb trace of 1 yd in length, will enable long casts to be made. The multiplier is not so suitable, being better employed in the early spring to chuck out heavily-weighted baits intended to be fished close to the river bed.

Many people cast a Toby upstream. This bait is certainly an excellent attractor but, oh dear, it is poor at hooking and landing salmon. You will find a method of improving the hooking capacity of the Toby in my earlier book. The Mepps is the favourite, in gold or copper. A size No. 4 is the usual choice.

Looking back through the diary it is apparent that this salmon of 12 June is the only one which has fallen to me on a Mepps as large as No. 5. Also, no other fish has come my way at Broadlands so freshly run that it carried sea lice.

It is quite interesting to analyse the Broadland fish which fell to my rod, fishing once a fortnight, between 1972 and 1977, and the manner of their taking. Twelve were on the fly, four on upstream Mepps, one on a Devon Yellow Belly minnow and eleven took the prawn. A total of 28 salmon and grilse at an average weight of 7.35 lb. Of these one was taken in March, two in June, and all the rest between 1 July and the end of the season in the first week of October.

A fly outfit for sea trout at night

June is the month when peal start to enter the rivers in noticeable numbers. It would be as well, before describing the fishing, to take a look at the equipment you need. A sea trout outfit varies little from the tackle you would take with you for trout on a lake or river, provided the items are not on the small or weak side. An 8 ft 6-in. trout rod for river dry fly is at the inadequate end of the available lengths. One of 9 ft is better, and 9 ft 6 in. is ideal. Those of 10 ft and 10 ft 6 in. are excellent for line and fish control but, even in carbon fibre, casting for several hours with such a weapon is very tiring and limited to those of strong build. Long distance casting is not a requirement at night; many peal are taken at between 10 and 15 yd. In consequence the rod may have an easy action, not soft, you understand. There must be the authority in the rod to direct the fish, but a stiff distance casting rod is unnecessary and may lead to hook hold being lost in the soft mouths of the peal.

The reel should be capable of holding a floating fly line, which is likely to be a No. 7, together with 50 or 60 yd of backing. It should not be less than 3½ in. in diameter, but 3⅝ in. or 3¾ in. would be better. A peal which takes out the whole fly line is an infrequent customer, but backing behind the fly line fills the spool, which, if of a large diameter, will make rapid line recovery. For the line itself, a floater, there is much to be said for a light colour, even white, at night. White by day is inadvisable in trout and salmon fishing, for the line flashes in the sky and scares fish. False casting for salmon, owing to the length of the rod is not often necessary; even so, one may feel uncomfortable with white. At night it is a different matter; a white or ice-blue fly line does not scare peal as there isn't enough light. In fact, to be able to see your line on the water surface is immensely helpful, for you have a pointer to the fly as it swings across the river in the dark. The position of plucking peal, those which tweak the fly, may be pinpointed – and tried again. It is also easier to locate a peal being played. For the leader, use the one described in Chapter 3 for wet flies and lures.

The net should have a bowframe, painted white or silver, with a diameter of not less than 20 in. This is the only style of fishing where one is grateful for the shiny brightness of the metal ring of some nets direct from the manufacturer –

you can guide the peal over the visible ring. Such a net will accommodate fish up to 7 lb with a reasonable margin of safety. We would all like to take larger nets with us – but are they a necessity? Perhaps on some rivers – you have to make up your own mind in the light of local fish sizes. I used to take a 22-in. Gye salmon net, but unslinging this for a 1-lb peal seemed ludicrous, and so a 20-in. net is now clipped to my belt. It is helpful if the handle of the net is the same length as your thigh waders then, if you wade with the net folded, and your hand on the hinge using the shaft as a staff, your hand will feel the water just before it would go over the top of your boots.

A torch, a priest on a string around your neck, a fish bass hanging from your belt to take peal whilst wading, midge cream, scissors and flies are all needed. Flies and fishing in the dark deserve a discourse of their own. Before becoming too technical let us return again to June, to those mellow sea trout evenings when we wait beside the river for the light to fade.

A shoal of hefty peal

21 June 1982. Dart. In the rough water at the top of Carradon Turn Pool. David took 1 sea trout of 3 lb and 3 more between 2 lb and 2½ lb each. On a Black Lure.

He telephoned me the next morning, 'Get down there tonight if you can. The place is stiff with them. Never known anything like it.' And the chances are, I thought to myself, he never will again in June. It is clear that it had rained quite a lot that week, for the diary of 19 June records a 1 lb 12-oz brown trout at 7.30 am on a 1¼-in. Black Dart whilst salmon fishing. Later, on 24 June a salmon of 8½ lb on a 1¼-in Hairy Mary The high water must have lasted for at least six days, and high water in the second half of June usually brings a run of substantial sea trout into the lower reaches of the river. All the same, you have to be lucky to arrive just as a group of large peal are passing. I have no knowledge of anyone habitually catching peal in the rough water at the head of Carradon Turn; certainly, that good fortune has not come my way. The tail end of the pool is normally the rich hunting ground. The season before last, 1986, I heard on the grapevine that one friend had experienced an equal bonanza in Nursery Pool, just above our boundary in June.

Good fortune has come my way in the month of June, but only with the occasional peal.

22 June 1984. Lara netted a good sea trout for me. Right in the narrow channel at the tail of The Manse. No. 8 Black Lure. 3 lb 3 oz.

Whilst fishing for trout in the river, in low water, one is always looking out for the first June shoals to arrive. Often there is disappointment on climbing trees to peer into the sunlit pools through polaroid glasses – in the first two or three weeks the lies are not yet occupied. Then, at the end of the month, there will come a day when you see a group of four or five grey, motionless, torpedo shapes; they look like grey wraiths, close to the river bed. Watching sea trout is almost as satisfactory as catching them. The longer you look, the more acute the scan, the greater will be your penetration of the secrets of the shadows and the sunlit gravel bed. Sooner or later a peal will move, twisting and turning, showing the flash of a silver flank not yet dulled by a long stay in fresh water. Sometimes he will make a circuit of the shoal and then, returning, settle again to await the movements of the night. There we will leave him, to plot his downfall in July.

CHAPTER 5

JULY

The month may be hot, bright and brassy by day, but for sea trout there is the dusk and the dawn and the near dark hours between. Through mid-summer twilight nights one stands alone under the stars, never in total darkness, sometimes wrapped in drifting mist, always hearing with clarity the sound of the running river and the call of the tawny owl. If you drive home before the night is out, in the early hours, there may be a badger trundling, snuffling along the road; a fox leaping a bank; and sheep and cows lying motionless, chewing, their nostrils expelling whispy flares of breath.

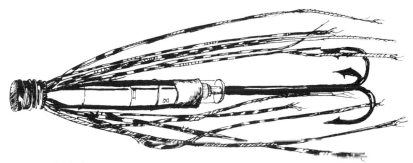

Silver stoat's tail

Sea trout may be taken by day from the Scottish lochs by dapping from a drifting boat – if there is a wind. Who would not return for such a holiday each year in Sutherland or Ross on jewelled waters between the mountain peaks? There is porridge and bacon and eggs for breakfast, cold sea trout sandwiches with cucumber and mayonnaise for an island lunch, and single malts with Gaelic names.

Rain is a help in taking grilse. Salmon, too, like a lift to river levels before they move, shaking off the torpor of warm water. Dawn and the final hour of day are the best times, when the sun lights only the tops of hills from the east and then, dipping, from the west. But if it rains you will be able to fish all the daylight hours. On a few dry fly rivers in the south of England the nymph is permitted from 1 July. The Pheasant Tail Nymph brings about the downfall of many trout. Those well-educated fellows who spurned the Imperial, the Wickham and the Wulff find out too late that all subsurface food is no longer innocent of hooks. Many leviathans succumb. There is the ten o'clock morning rise, a pint of quenching ale at half-past-twelve and cricket on the wireless after lunch. The evening is the time when wise old trout move with some abandon: sipping, swirling, bulging and rising at spinners and sedges drifting or fluttering in the fading light. On trout still waters there are problems if it is hot and sunny: it is too bright; the water is too warm; the algae is thick and green; and weed grows to choke the open places. The trout then take refuge in the depths. Even so some anglers are achievers. These fishers use sinking lines and large lures trickled over the bottom of the lake for the trout which have descended in search of both food and cool water. Some fish their flies at dusk.

Sea trout at night

24 July 1983. Dart. A night for Lara to remember. Aged 15 years, the first time out for peal. On a No. 8 Black Lure in top of Carradon Ford 12 oz and a beauty of 2 lb which took out much of her line. I had 3 more of 12 oz, 1 lb, and 1 lb 12 oz. Same fly. 2 in Abbot's Mead, 1 in tail of Carradon Ford.

37 *A 2-lb peal* (24 July 1983)

You really need a helper on your first night out for peal. Many are attracted to try the fish by its wild fighting spirit, elusive nature, and the delicate flavour when presented upon a plate, but it is no good trying to fish in the dark unless you are already competent by day. When you are able to cast out a dry fly accurately at a rising trout without becoming caught up behind, play him with calm control, and tie on a fly with practised fingers, you are ready to take up peal fishing. You should also have a knowledge of the river bed: the boulders, trenches, sunken logs, and the sandy banks on which it is safe to stand at night. A daytime reconnaissance should be made.

On the night of 24 July we sat under the bank at the tail of Abbot's Mead waiting for the light to go. It is never easy, waiting, but to start too soon will spoil your chances in the smooth glides at the tails of pools. So, wait until the colours fade out of the flowers, until the far bank is a dark shadow and distances are hard to judge. There is no need to be idle whilst you wait. If it is your first night tie on a single-hooked fly for this is less likely to tangle on the leader than the treble of a tube fly. One fly only should also be your rule; droppers cause troubles in the dark. Rub the leader down with 'sink mix', then take the rod, with line, leader and fly attached to the river edge to let the fly and leader soak in the water until it is time to start. The first few casts should not be spoiled by a leader floating on the water surface – fly and nylon must sink at once. Rub your neck, face, ears, hands and wrists with midge cream and then sit down quietly to watch and listen. Birds fly up the valley to roost; sometimes a flotilla of mallard ducklings, led by the softly chiding duck, drift and paddle downstream – you must move them on in case they decide to spend the night where you intend to fish. Bats flit by, gathering insects from the cooling air between the trees, above the river and over the grasses of the meadow at your back. Then a peal jumps, a vertical bar of silver leaps straight up and then smacks down, sending waves across the pool. Very startling, this welcome intrusion on silence and solitude, but where he jumped was no surprise. If you know the river then you know where they will jump, and where they leap they often take. There are places where peal jump but do not take, no matter how they are tried, or how often, on however many nights. Why this rejection is so may remain a mystery for a season or more, but will probably be solved one night if you try them in a different way, casting from another angle, altering the depth or speed of retrieve, or some other factor. Many of the jumping peal in July are small, weighing 1 lb or less; these are usually in the shallow places. The hefty peal, the 2-, 3- and 4-pounders, prefer 3 or 4 ft of water over their backs and are sometimes caught by your casting upstream into these deeper places.

The light has gone, it is time to start. On Lara's first night in this pool we waded together and shared a rod. Out we went, hands on each other's shoulders for co-ordination and added balance – there are slippery boulders on the river bed. No stumbling, no clattering studded boots – a silent ghostlike progress to the place from which to cast. Two or three pulls of line from the reel, two false casts and then the fly went out at 45° across the river before dropping onto the dark surface. The line swung around in the current to hang downstream. Another yard was drawn off the clicking spool before the fly was cast out at the same angle to swim again across the river. This time a small retrieve was made with the free hand, the line controlled over the forefinger of the hand on the butt of the rod. Then straight across – and a peal took. The take may be gentle, a soft halt to the passage of the fly, you raise the rod and there he is – fighting in a flurry of spray. Sometimes the take is a hard jerk – but there is no fear with an 8- or 9-lb point.

The first peal that night was the one of 1 lb 12 oz which I hooked before handing over the rod to Lara. 'Keep the rod tip high. Let him run if he wishes. He's over there! When he's tired he'll turn on his side to show a silver flank.' I unclipped the net from the hook on my belt. In time he surrendered, to be drawn over the white rimmed net and lifted clear of the water. Lara hit him on the head with the priest before unhooking, whilst still in the net. She then let him slide into the bass which hung from my waist. We tried for another, casting upstream, down river, and across, but without success before wading out and walking up the river bank to Carradon Ford. At the top of the pool, on our knees, for the moon and a clear sky were behind us, Lara cast her Black Lure under the beech trees which line the opposition's bank. First throw a tiny peal took; 12 oz may not be much, but it was a start, and who returns the first peal of their life? Leaving her, I moved away to fish 20 yards downstream when she called and a peal splashed in front of my new position. 'That's mine. He keeps on running. I can't stop him. Will he ever come back?.' In five minutes she had the better of the fight, the net slid under him and we admired a perfect 2-pounder by torchlight and the moon. Two more came my way whilst wading in the run-off whilst she sat, tired but fulfilled behind me on the bank. Even when the fish are on the take there comes a time when enough is enough. Your shoulders and back ache and your step falters. Go home whilst success still glows, taking with you your supper for tomorrow night. Tomorrow? It's hard to realize tomorrow is today.

Night sea-trout-flies

I urge you to err on the side of a large fly rather than go for something small. A No. 8 single in clear water, or a No. 6 if there is colour in the flow. A No. 4 is taking matters too far – not in length but in leverage on the hook hold and possibly in weight. If you need a long fly, then make up a two-hooked tandem lure. There are a number of books which describe how this may be done, and the dressings of suitable patterns. The Black Lure, Alexandra and the Teal and Silver Blue are amongst the best of sea trout flies – start with these and avoid tandems and treble hooks until you have fished for a night or two without tangles in the leader.

It is hard to say whether there is any advantage in fishing a socketed treble-hooked tube at night, although they certainly have a place in my box. However skilled you become, there will be occasions when the nylon of the leader becomes jammed between the three hooks of the treble. Unaware of this you may continue casting – regular checks must be made. But the fat socketed tube has a place, particularly in heavier cloudy water –it may be that the disturbance in the water flow caused by such a fly draws the attention of the peal. My favourite tubes are the Silver Stoat's Tail and the Alexandra: dress both with flat silver tinsel for the body

It would be satisfactory to record that well-waterproofed, bushy, dry flies, skidding on the surface as they swing to hang below your position, take as many peal as the wet fly and sub-surface lure. Satisfactory because it is heart stopping in the dim light to see the peal take. Dry fly for trout, floating fly line for salmon, the surface lure for sea trout, they are all more exciting than fishing deep down where you cannot see the take. Excitement is not everything – you want peal in the bass – and the surface lure at night does not put so many there as the fly fished just under the water. That is my experience. Some waters may be different and others anglers achieve great success.

The Pheasant Tail Nymph

Clamp tight on a No. 12 single hook with your fly tying vice. From head to tail wind on fine copper wire, with extra turns near to the head to form the thorax of the nymph. Take a tail feather of a cock pheasant from the store you set aside after a January shoot and cut out eight long fibres. Tie these in at the tail with the copper wire with the fibre points free and pointing to the rear by 1/4 in. Wind the wire up to the head, wind the fibres over the wire and up the body to the eye of the hook where they are secured by two turns of the wire. Double back the fibres over the thorax and tie down, lay them forward once more, tie in, trim off and secure the wire with four whipped turns. Time: three minutes. Product: a nymph which will take trout from 8 oz to 8 lb.

13 July 1979. River Kennet. Hungerford Fishery. Bill and I had a very good day. Eight rainbows, six on Pheasant Tail Nymph, one on a Daddy Long Legs and one on a mayfly. Total weight 16 lb 8 oz. Two best trout 3 lb 12 oz and 3 lb 6 oz. 4X leaders.

Each year Bill asks me to fish the Kennet, and the Dunn which runs parallel to the main river. The choice of day is left open. 'Come when you can. How about July? The nymph is allowed from the first day of the month.'

July is my choice, for nymph fishing is fascinating in a river if one finds and stalks a trout. You must wear polaroid glasses to see the fish as they lie one or two feet down, waiting for the food brought by this bountiful river. With practice and experience you will soon catch on to the skills of finding fish. First of all work your way upriver, approaching the trout from behind, moving slowly. In fact, you hardly need move at all, for almost all the water holds fish – all you have to do, as a first step, is to spot one. Sit still on a bench and watch,

38 *Eight rainbows – six were taken on a Pheasant Tail Nymph. River Kennet* (13 July 1979)

still and silent; sooner or later a trout will give himself away.

As one moved up the Dunn, from Peart's trout farm, there were some fine thick-trunked willow trees on the opposite bank. Trees on the other side cut out reflection on the water, enabling us to see trout in the shadows of the trunks. They were a great help, those trees, until someone cut them down! Up you wander, peering into the shadows, with water-piercing glance searching the river bed, attending to the yard or two in front of a bar of weed, but not fishing until you find a fish. Then you think you see one, and move back a step to confirm the sighting, a grey shadow with a square end to the tail. The trout may help you make up your mind by opening his mouth to reveal the white edges of the jaws. The nymph is on the point; kneel, keep back from the bank and cast a yard or two above his position. The copper nymph drifts downstream, sinking as it goes. Then lift the rod, inducing him to take when your creation is before his nose. If he approaches the nymph and opens his mouth, tighten at once. By the time you have raised your rod he will have shut his mouth on the hook. Sometimes the nymph drifts past him, ignored, and then he turns and gives chase. An exhilarating moment but don't let anticipation freeze your hands; keep the nymph moving, if it loses life the trout will turn away.

There are times when it is impossible to see into the water, but you notice the movements of a feeding trout. He may be cruising, shrimping, bulging, nymphing – here one moment, five yards away the next. Such a fish sets problems to be solved. If you cast blindly in his direction he may be frightened by the line. He may swim by, going downstream, just below your bank; keep still and he may take no exception to your presence. Do not hurry to catch this trout. Retreat from the river to watch, try to discern a pattern to his movements, for if there is a pattern his arrival may be anticipated, the nymph cast ahead and tweaked to life at the crucial moment. Many trout have fallen in this way. Then there is the 'black hole'. 'The nylon slid forward and down – into the black hole', anglers say with a far away look in the eye. The method is simple and satisfactory – use it when you know where a stationary trout is feeding, are almost certain of his position, but cannot make him out. Tie on a 9-ft knotless tapered leader of 4X and grease the yard closest to the line, leaving the two yards leading to the point. Attach your copper-bodied nymph, draw off line from the reel, judge the distance with a false cast and pitch the nymph two yards above the estimated lie. The nymph is gone, the nylon too is below the water surface film – all you can see is the greased yard, drifting down towards you. Then the yard slides forward –into the black hole. Raise the rod to tighten, for a trout is on the other end.

16 July 1976. River Kennet. Hungerford. An outstanding trout. 7½-lb rainbow. 3X leader. Pheasant Tail Nymph. Had probably escaped from a pond which had not been used for 2 or 3 years on Peart's trout farm. Had to jump in and follow the trout downstream.

If you go up the carrier that runs past the house in which Lancelot Peart lived, leaving the Duffer's Pool on your left, you will come to the scene where this trout was fooled and defeated. His demise came about in this way. A trout had risen over the far side of the stream. I then watched the place for ten minutes, trying to make out his exact location for an accurate throw. I peered through the rushes on my side, eyes focussed on the water as it swirled under the far bank. Failing to find the trout my gaze relaxed and there, unsought, almost under my feet was the grey back of the largest trout I'd seen in my life. Bill came by, walking lightly, as far as possible from the river. He wanted his lunch as much as I wanted that trout. The trout would have to wait. Over sausages, eggs and chips in one of the inns of the town we plotted his downfall. Returning to the river, the 4X was replaced by a 3X leader, the Pheasant Tail Nymph tied on, and the rod pushed forward. He was still there, just below the surface, and not at all excited or disturbed. In went the nymph three yards upstream, out of sight behind the rushes. The grey back eased forward, the tail waved, the trout moved out of sight. I raised the rod in hope, and he was on. Down the river we went, down and down, in the water over welly tops to skirt around the trees. We almost reached the Duffer's. Out came my dreadful net, one of those spreading 'Y'-shaped contraptions which have to be untangled to be set. A gardener mowing grass moved forward to assist, a helpful unthinking gesture of support which scared the trout to renewed effort. Eventually, he was netted head first with the tail drooping out of the bag.

Kingfisher

The wake fly for trout

31 July 1981. Fernworthy. James caught 2 rainbows on a large White Muddler on the surface, used as a wake fly. Douglas and Simon 1 each by the same method

The wake lure may be fished up or down on a river, if both methods are allowed, and by casting out and stripping in at speed on a lake. Success depends on attracting the trout through disturbance and curiosity by the creation of a rippling trail. A fat muddler with a bucktail head is a practical choice, for deer hair tends to float. Waterproof the fly by placing it in the neck of your floatant bottle, with the hook over the rim, give several shakes, remove and allow to dry completely. In a lake, cast out as far as you are able, then strip in at speed. Trout come with a rush and hook themselves – sometimes they lose courage and swirl away at the final moment. The method works if there is a slight ripple but is not so good in a heavy wave; nothing is caught in a flat calm. This style also succeeds without intention on rivers, with small flies, as the result of an across-river cast when, after the drift, the fly starts to drag around downstream.

Droppers or bob flies should be used similarly in lakes or lochs from bank or boat. In the final stages of the retrieve each fly is raised into view from below the surface, then trickled across the water before the final lift-off by the angler. On still waters a long rod helps. The longer the rod the further out may the scuttling commence. Success is more likely if there is deep water close to the bank when fishing from the shore – trout refuse to follow into the shallow water of a gently shelving bank. The best place to employ the bob fly is on the bank where the wind blows down the edge, parallel with the shore. The cast may be made straight out, retrieved as usual in the initial stages then, when raising the rod, the bob approaches the bank in a curve, the line being bellied out by the wind and waves.

11 July 1980. Upper Tamar Lake. 5 rainbows. 7 lb 1 oz. Fish were rising steadily to midge pupa but would not take an artificial nymph. These trout caught by attracting them with a deer's hair sedge as dropper stripped across the surface. Attracted by this they took the Black Muddler on the point.

It is a fact that trout will rush to the surface after a wake fly or dropper. It is equally true that after being brought close by curiosity, they won't always take – the trout swirls and turns away. If, at the moment of rejection, a sub-surface fly or lure appears, he will often take this second chance, particularly if the fly is of a different pattern. This happened on 11 July, when I put a deer's hair sedge as dropper and Black Muddler on the point; alternatively, I could have used a Gold Muddler on the dropper and a Black & Peacock Spider at the leader's end. The combinations are endless.

Catching trout in hot weather

Long hot spells often arrive and last for two or three weeks in July. After several days, or a couple of weeks of such a period you rise from bed in trepidation. With annoyance you note that a bright sun is shining without pity from a clear blue sky. Trout may still be caught in such conditions, but only by cunning forethought.

Consider the river and the needs of the trout in hot weather: cool water, oxygen and food. The trout are there, they have to eat and they have to breathe. The necessities make them vulnerable. In a chalk stream it is really only sensible to fish in the early morning or at dusk. In the evening the trout come up when the sun has gone down below the horizon. Not only has the sun disappeared but food has come on the scene – sedges are hatching. Trout love a sedge, particularly the caperer. The hour before darkness sets in is a magic one – fish rise in many places. Even so, do not expect to find the fishing easy. It is a memorable achievement to take a brace at dusk, in the final quarter hour. You could catch a river trout in a heat wave by day if allowed to sink the fly, for they will be in the deeps, in the cool retreats. If you must fish by day go to the bubbling rushing places where trout have gone for oxygen and cover. Tie on the copper dressed Pheasant Tail Nymph and cast it up into the rough water ahead, just at the edge of the current, perhaps below a weir, and fish each throw back towards you in little pulls and draws. You cannot see the trout but they will see the nymph and maybe one will take.

39 *Tony Schofield nets a brown trout of 1 lb 4 oz at Fernworthy (28 July 1987)*

40 *Tom Brown shows there is more than one way to land a wild moorland trout on No. 14 Red Sedge* (23 July 1987)

When running a fishing course in these hot spells a moorland river or stream often rescues us from a blank day if the flow is fast and bubbly. At least there is water movement, a changing scene, and the chance of a trout around the next bend in the valley. Rivers are winding waters of hope, varied and full of surprises. However bright the day on Dartmoor, there is always a chance with a dry fly cast up amongst the rocks. Go for the deep gaps between the boulders – there is shade in these places, and moorland trout are almost always hungry. In the bright conditions you must fish fine, a 5X or 6X leader.

23 July 1987. Dart. Wickham's Fancy. Kite's Imperial and Red Sedge. No. 14 hooks. 6 Brown trout to Tom, Anthony and Andrew. All boys under 14 years old. Beached the trout on gravel and the rocks

Hot though they are, thigh boots should be worn when you creep up the river, wading, low down and out of sight. Cast a short line, bounce the fly off the edge of a boulder, drop it on the other side of a rock and strike like lightning if there is a rise. You must jump up at once on hooking brownies under these conditions to close with them. Keep the leader 'up and down'. Played from a distance you are bound to be snagged when he dives under a rock. A short rod puts one at a disadvantage, a 9 ft helps place the fly correctly and keep a trout away from trouble when hooked.

A heat wave on a reservoir may be dealt with in two ways: fish a floating line at the beginning and the end of the day; sink your fly close to the bed of the lake at other times. The evening rise may be fished with a sedge fly on the top or an Invicta just below the surface. Even in a flat calm, in the final light, in the reflection of the sun's last glow, you may take a trout. Personally, I like to put out a dry sedge whilst the light remains then; when the fly can no longer be seen, I change to an Invicta. Do not try to tie the wet fly to the end of your fine leader – at dusk, nylon will not be clearly visible and precious minutes will be wasted. Instead, have a second leader ready, a heavier 3X, on a spare rod. The final 15 minutes should not be missed through fiddling with tackle for they may be your only chance of a brace. As the light faded, I once made the mistake of changing the No. 12 dry fly on a 5X point for a No. 8 Green Sedge Pupa, still on the same fine nylon – there were three solid takes and the leader broke three times.

You don't have to rise early or go to bed late in order to catch lake trout in a heat wave. Trout may be taken, on and off, throughout the daylight hours, by fishing a sinking line to take the lure down to the bed of the lake. There is a proviso – the area you choose to fish must be deep enough, and therefore cool enough, to shelter the trout. If fishing from a gently shelving bank it will need a long throw to reach the deep area, a pause of 10 or 15 seconds to allow the line to sink, followed by the retrieve. To reach trout in a deep area you may need a boat.

Teaching someone to fish for trout on a reservoir in bright hot weather can be a depressing business. Conditions are all wrong; you know this and so does the

41 *Graham Allison, 'The Dean from Harvard', cleans his trout*

pupil, and the trout are not inclined to help. The learner cannot be sure your advice is sound without a catch to prove ability. Do not lose heart. Instead, find a stream running into the reservoir and go there, for the trout will be in residence, in the coolness of the aerated water. Many times the north burn at Fernworthy has saved me from a fishless day. In the summer of 1987 the telephone rang, 'Would I take out Graham Allison, Dean of John F. Kennedy School of Government, Harvard University.' We fished all morning at Fernworthy without result. He was very good about it, but something had to be done. Taking him to the burn we changed the line to a fast sinking Wet Cel 2, attached a No. 8 Black Chenille and cast out a long line where the stream runs into the lake. In this manner Graham took a brown before we sat down to lunch. Now, if you leave a water undisturbed, trout start to forage and explore, becoming bold. In the bed of this stream you can see many sedge pupae – fat tasty meals. There are also shoals of trout fry. Suddenly, where lake met stream, there was a wallop – not a rise, not a delicate sip, but a slap as a greedy trout turned. 'You see that sand bank, where the water deepens, just behind that rock. That's where we'd take a 'bow [a rainbow trout] in the States,' he said. The Dean forgot the Russians, the ayatollahs, John F. Kennedy and the balance of power; all he wanted was that trout. That's what fishing does to you – puts things in correct perspective. He crept forward, on his knees, and to my astonishment plopped the fly over the rock which separated him from his quarry. They were not two yards apart. The English brownie, knowing all about the importance of the Atlantic Alliance, and anxious to do its bit, helped himself.

At Tamar Lake, on the border of Devon and Cornwall, there is a stream which runs in at the top of the bay on the east, or Devon, side. You will take a trout there in a heatwave with a lure fished off a sinking line. A killing attractor for this game is the Appetizer, a most unlikely looking white fluffy lure when dry. Wet, it is as close to a trout fry as one could wish. Fish this in the cool depths of this stream and, sooner or later, a brownie or rainbow will be attracted. Although brown trout are no longer stocked in this water, considerable efforts are made to provide them, the wild ones, with suitable spawning grounds. Tractors take trailer loads of gravel to the streams to improve the beds and trout take full advantage of this in their winter spawning. In consequence, in the summer, you are likely to take a 1- or 2-lb brownie on the Appetizer. If the appearance of this lure repels you, then try a No. 10 Sweeney Todd on the point and a No. 12 Black & Peacock Spider as a dropper. Some years back, on three consecutive Wednesdays, I took rainbows of over 3 lb on the Black & Peacock, fished in this manner there.

Finally, the following entries of a hot week may bring you hope:

13 July 1983. Newhouse Fishery [a lake]. A very successful first day in appalling heat. All fish deep as water hot. Andrew had a limit of 4, including a best of 2 lb 8 oz. Richard had a good brown and 2 rainbows. I had 4. Total 9 rainbows, 2 brown. 15 lb 6 oz.

and:

14 July. River Lyd. Anthony had a brown trout on a dry Wickham's Fancy, his first trout. Richard had 1 as well. On the Dart in the evening Amos caught 3 browns on a March Brown fished wet, Anthony had another, and so did Richard, and Andrew, 1 in the dark.

and:

15 July. Dart. We had 6 brown trout on wet flies and dry Wickhams.

finally:

17 July. Dart. Carradon Ford by the pipe and tail of Carradon Turn. 3 small peal on a No. 8 Black Lure. Total 3 lb 12 oz. Midnight to 1.00 am.

From these entries the tactics are clear:
• fish in the cool depths of a lake (Newhouse)
• fish in a shady river (the Lyd has a canopy of trees)
• fish a rough, well aerated river (Dart)
• fish at night for peal

Grilse and salmon

The month of July sees the start of the main grilse run into the lower reaches of rivers, and the appearance of considerable numbers of the earlier large spring fish higher up the valley. Of course, the arrival of both in their respective areas may depend on rain to lift the river to a fish running level, and provide sufficient water for them to jump the weirs and ascend the salmon ladders. We are all fortunate that the main grilse run commences at the start of the holiday season – many anglers will take the night train to Inverness and from there go on to the West Coast of Scotland. Much grilse fishing will be done from boats on lochs connected to the sea, and sea trout also will be taken in these waters. In rivers, throughout these weeks, 4-, 5- and 6-lb grilse will appear high up the valley if there is a flood – these fish run far and fast on a spate to catch up with the earlier heavier fish. They catch up in July and from then on large and small salmon take the fly, from 4 to 14 lb and even more.

6 July 1986. Dart. Grilse 5 lb. 10.30 am in tail of second stickle below Broken Hook Pool. Also at noon, 12 lb. Tail of Narrow Run. A strong fish which jumped three times. 1 in. Black Dart tube. A passer-by took photographs with my camera. Mark and I rose a fish three times the day before in the Saucepan Pool where Mark photographed the fish as it came up to the fly.

It is clear from this entry covering two days that there was a long spate which brought in the grilse. Many times you fish over a length of water without result and then, on returning two hours later, take a fish. That was the way on 6 July. A change from dourness to a willing attitude may be due to a number of factors, singly or in combination. The clearing of heavy colour as the water level recedes; the sun going behind a cloud; a shower; the start of a stiff breeze, the advent of evening. At times one cannot pinpoint the factor; at others the cause of co operation is obvious.

Only once before had I hooked a salmon in the lie of this grilse – and that salmon came off after ten minutes. A single hook, a No. 4 Thunder & Lightning, was to blame. When you hook or rise a salmon the place is marked indelibly upon the brain and thereafter, in passing, the lie is given a cast. Well, this time, after a gap of several years, there was a fish at home. The lie is one to which one casts a long line downstream, right at the tail of a stickle which has bushes on our bank. When he is hooked you are unable to go down river to close with him; he must come up to you. To persuade a fish to come upriver is not usually a matter of great difficulty, provided he does not become excited. Keeping him calm is up to you: no sideways pressure with the rod; no sudden shocks; no lifting; just a gentle pull, almost a beckoning. He followed and through the stickle we went; up between a fast and narrow gap to the pool above and there the net trapped him. On the bank I doubled him head to tail with a length of twine, wetted him with a dip in the river, and slid him into my inside pocket. The large interior pocket of a waxproof jacket will hold a grilse, or even two, or accept a 10-lb fish. A bit of a squash perhaps, but better carrying a salmon this way than constantly putting them down on the river bank as one fishes on, up or down the river.

The second, the 12-pounder, came an hour and a half later on the same lure. Home-dressed flies, (I tie my own Black and Copper Dart tubes) are durable, often accounting for three or four salmon. Not so the treble hook. However fine the quality of a treble, and Partridge are amongst the best, a hook may be strained in playing a salmon. The netting is the moment of greatest stress. One of the hooks may be weakened, particularly if the salmon has been lip-hooked, or a point has been caught in the nylon net mesh. Put this used treble back in an empty compartment of the fly box, take it home and consign it to the dustbin – far better to pay for new hooks for they cost little, than to lose a salmon owing to an opened hook. The 12-pounder had to be given a great deal of stick for he was strong and angry. He also made use of the current, which is fast and powerful in that narrow place. There was little in my favour with one small indentation in the bank for the netting, and that bay no more than a yard or two across. Worse still this slack puddle is inconsiderately placed at the run-off – you draw him towards the net and towards the best line of escape. In moments like this I am always astonished at the extent to which a fly rod will bend, be it split cane or carbon fibre. To take this salmon I entered the water to the top of, and just over, my thigh boots. The rod almost cracked, and in he came. The leader was of 15-lb breaking strain – and I was glad that I had not used anything lighter.

4 July 1979. Dart. Right at top of Narrow Run, beside stone. Low water. 4.30 pm when sun off pool by tree shadows. 8½ lb. Hooked on 1-in Black Dart. Played by Bill, netted by myself.

Salmon usually edge up to the top, or neck, of a pool as the river falls to a low level. They seek cover and aeration in the bubbling flow. At such a place you may take a fish if the lie is protected from the sun. The fly was a 1-in. Black Dart, which may seem large in low, and almost certainly in clear water. There can be considerable variation in the length and amount of orange bucktail tied around the circumstance of any tube fly – you may please yourself. Additionally, in low water a heavily dressed specimen may have some of the bucktail fibres trimmed out at the head whilst at the waterside, resulting in a sparse fly. Do not trim the length of the fibres; a crew cut looks stubby. The fibres should finish at the hook bend in their natural fine tapered points.

Grilse on the upstream Mepps

14 July 1976. Test. Broadlands. Longbridge Pool. 3.00 pm. Upstream No. 4 Mepps. 6-lb grilse. Also 5.30 pm Hospital Pool. Upstream No. 4 Mepps. 4½-lb sea trout.

Longbridge Pool may be fished from either bank. On this occasion I was fishing from the left, just upstream of the bridge by Bernard Aldrich's fishing hut. As you can see, it was nearly time for tea, which Bernard brewed in the hut on a gas cooker. The hut at tea-time is a meeting place where the adventures of the day are discussed and the record book examined. No doubt I was fishing near the hut in anticipation of my tea. The first fish was slim, shapely and a silver colour; the flanks of grilse glint and reflect the light when straight up from the sea. The sea trout came later to the same bait, further down the river. I think it was the only sea trout I caught at Broadlands and, when it took, I thought it was a grilse at first. On the bank the hunched shoulder, forward eye, square tail and small scales made clear the true identity.

Reconnaissance for sea trout fishing

15 July 1984. Dart. Tail of Carradon Ford. Mid-river. 2 lb 7-oz peal. No. 8 Black Lure. Midnight.

'What on earth is he doing up there?', a watcher might question as I scramble up a tree in waders, aged nearly 60. Trees by sea trout pools are a double asset: they provide shade and cover for the peal, giving them a sense of security; and they afford a look-out support to me. Until you know the river really well you can learn a lot by visiting the sea trout pools by day and climb up a tree to look out for peal through polaroid glasses.

On that day a line of peal, in as close a formation as migrating greylag geese, was visible in the middle of the river. Nothing very remarkable about that if they had not been in the place to which I wade before starting to cast. On previous nights I must have been treading on some of the fish. On 15 July, in the dark, I crept up to the bank, lowered myself into the water to cut out silhouette and stayed down, just below the stinging nettles! Several upstream casts later, from my normal standing place which was being searched by the fly, this peal took and ran away upriver. I was very worried when he leapt two or three times at the end of his run as peal often leap at the end of a run, sometimes throwing the hook before turning downstream. He then rushed back to me and came to the net. That first rush is the telling time – they rarely do it twice.

Another, deeper place, further down the river is the haunt of heavy peal and the occasional salmon. When I first took that beat on the river one of the pleasures was to approach the place from behind a bush which overhung the water. During the day I would peep through the leaves of the bush to take a good look into the dark water beneath. The peal there were large, wide mouthed and square tailed. There was never a small one in that group. A small stream runs into the side of the pool, cascading over the bank onto a small ledge at water level where I took my stand and started to fish. The peal were there, for I had seen them that afternoon. All was quiet, the casting clean, the point of the Teal & Blue was sharp, at any moment . . . , then the waterfall started to fill up my boots. Forgetting the fly, which sank to the river bed, I had to attend to my wet feet. Later, lifting the rod the fly stuck on the bottom, resisting my retrieve, and then the river bed moved. Over to the far side went the fish, the pressure increased on the leader, he swirled under a tree on the opposite bank, then set off up the pool. On and on, regardless of the drag, he took out line and then leaped twice, glinting, reflecting, shining in the moon. The crashes and suspense were awful – then he was gone. The fly came back. Salmon, grilse or hefty peal? It remains a mystery.

An expedition to Scotland for grilse and sea trout

In the evening of 7 July 1987 Mark Owen came to me on the Dart to polish up his Spey casting before a holiday in Scotland. Later, as it grew dark, we sat beside the river waiting to set about the sea trout. He told me that he would be fishing the Ewe in Ross and Cromarty the following week and accepted a roll of black and white film, promising to take some photographs of the action. Subsequently he unfolded details of a day and night of fishing with his companion, Sandy Muirhead.

The night:
16 July 1987. River Ewe. Scatwell Estate. Tee Pool. 7 finnock. One sea trout 4½ lb. No. 8 Silver Wilkinson.

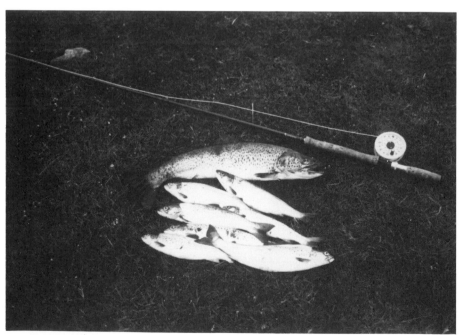

42 *Seven finnock and one 4½-lb sea trout. River Ewe (16 July 1987)*

1 Fishing the Dart

3 Fishing the Dart

2 A wild brown trout from the Lyd

4 Stocking trout at Tamar Lake

5 Reaching out on Dartmoor

6 Playing a trout

7 Netting an October rainbow from the Test

8 Boys cleaning trout at Fernworthy

9 Playing a grilse taken on a fly

10 The Findhorn in Scotland – scene of James Stuart's 'Hairy Mary' adventure
with the lady from Kentucky

11 Taking a trout from the Kennet

12 Landing trout

43 *Sandy plays a 6-lb grilse taken on a No. 8 Tosh double. River Ewe (18 July 1987)*

They fished with a 10 ft 6-in. fly rod, using a white floating line which showed up on the water in the dark, and a 9-lb leader. They also took a 9 ft 3-in. rod with a sinking line to fish a sunk lure in the darkest part of the night. It doesn't get very dark so far north in mid-summer, and fishing did not begin until 11.00 pm. The cream of the action often takes place between 11.00 pm and 1.00 am. Not so on this occasion – not a pluck, not a splash, or even a pull until much later, at 3.00 am. Then followed 30 minutes of take after take. Tiring it may be to hang on so late, but there is always a dram before bed to soothe taut muscles and relax the eyes in sleep.

The day:
18 July 1987. River Ewe. Sea Pool. Scatwell. 9.30 am. 6-lb grilse. No. 8 Tosh double. Sandy Muirhead. 1.30 pm. 9-lb salmon to Mark. Same fly in Hen Pool.

The day was warm and dry with a strong upstream wind when they started to fish at 8.00 am. The river ran at a good summer level, and the current was strong and swirling. There had been rain 48 hours before, but only a freshener, not enough to raise the river level. Sandy fished down and across in the conventional manner, holding a loop of free line between the fingers. There was a touch, he let go of the loop, raised the rod, and there he stood, up to his knees, fighting it out in the river. Mark's came later, after lunch; it was a heavier salmon of 9 lb, which gave him a run for his money, helped by the strength of the river.

Mark told me that in previous seasons they had also taken sea trout from the river by day. They achieved this by casting a dry fly upstream from the end of a croy jutting out into the river. They didn't use a large dry fly such as the sort you would tie on for the dap, or a small one such as those for the chalk streams of the south; instead they chose a medium-sized one. The fly had to be well hackled, waterproofed and fished off a 6-lb point. So far as he could remember, the fly had been a No. 10 Grey Wulff. It was a holiday after anyone's heart: purple heather, the hills and clouds, a farmhouse in which to sleep, single malts and sea trout suppers.

Thunderstorms

11 July 1982. Dart. In a thunderstorm with much lightning. Myself at 11.30 pm. One sea trout of 1 lb 4 oz in tail of Abbot's Mead. Teal & Silver Blue.

Without doubt, it is very dangerous to fish with a carbon fibre rod in a thunderstorm as it conducts lightning; you can be killed or at the least stunned and severely burnt if you are hit by a flash. It is even more unwise to be wading, for you can then be knocked down and drown whilst unconscious. In 1982 I fished during that storm because I had driven 30 miles to the river and was using a 9 ft 6-in split-cane rod, and had persuaded myself that this was safe in comparison with carbon fibre. I don't think my theory was correct because although the rod was wooden, both it and the line were wet. Today my night peal fishing in rivers is done with a carbon fibre rod, which is so much lighter than split cane; as a result the rod *has* to be put down until an electric storm has passed, as carbon is an excellent conductor.

Following this modernization of tackle I found myself unable to fish one night in August 1987. On arrival at the river there were promises of good things to come: a large peal sploshed several times at the head of the pool, several salmon moved, and school peal popped up all over the place as the light faded. Then the sky darkened, and stars were blotted out, rain fell and lightning flashed. You can put up with rain, turn up your collar, pull down your hat, and wait for the disturbance to pass, but there has to be a wind to move a storm. That night was calm and the storm sat over the valley with the lightning and thunder appearing to move in a circle overhead. After two hours in which my fly did not touch the water I gave up and went home.

On the subject of electricity and overhead powerlines, the newspapers regularly record the deaths of anglers electrocuted through their long carbon fibre fly rods or coarse fishing poles when these touch overhead cables. Live cables cross our river just above a good sea trout lie. It is as well in such a situation to go to the place by day, cast as one would at night, and check that there is absolutely no chance of your fly rod or line touching the cable when you return at night. Only when this has been done can you fish with peace of mind.

So far as trout and salmon are concerned, you should welcome a thunderstorm for stimulating the fish. Start to fish as soon as the storm has passed. It may be the roll of the thunder and the shaking of the earth, or perhaps the heavy raindrops oxygenating the water unleashing additional fish energy, I don't know. Whatever reason, after the sky clears and the atmospheric pressure starts to rise, the fish start to take. As with salmon, so also with trout and the insects upon which they feed. This is particularly noticeable at mayfly time if you shelter in a hut which looks out on the river where the raindrops splatter upon the surface. When the storm has passed a fly or two hatch out, then several more, and trout start to rise until the river is alive with feeding fish. Swallows and swifts are quickly on the scene, and it is sad if one of these takes your artificial fly as the cast unfurls and the bird collapses into the river. This has happened twice to me. Each time I have carefully drawn the bird across the surface, removed the hook and put the little feathery bundle up somewhere to dry, but I doubt that it survives the shock. A swift which has landed on grass is not able to take off again – his legs are so short and his wings so long. Swallows and housemartins are able to take wing from the ground where they land to collect mud for their nests and, I believe, grit for their crops. A swift has no nesting material so does not need to land on the ground. If a swift is found in long grass due to some accident he may be picked up and thrown into the air – they usually catch their balance at once and streak away.

The Specimen Trout – a short story

Giles felt the sunny light of early morning from behind his eyelids. He opened them as he lay relaxed and warm to look at the blue sky beyond the bedroom window, whilst contentment spread through his limbs, for today he would go fishing. There were two weeks ahead of him, a length of time which could at first be squandered; towards the end he savoured every daylight hour. He respected the trout fishing knowledge of his grandfather, with whom he spent the holiday on the edge of the moor. Grandpa rarely called him Giles, just 'boy'. 'Now boy,' he would say at breakfast, 'which stream will you fish today?'. The old man had not left the zeal of youth behind in his journey through life, and as the boy unfolded the plan for the day the grandfather could see it all come true: the red spots on the flanks of the little moorland trout the boy would catch; the Blue Upright fly dancing down towards him on the rippling stream. He felt again the temptation of the wriggling worm which could be kicked from under a dried up cowpat. Grandpa knew that Giles considered him old, but to himself his years had passed too quickly for him to feel his age.

Giles hid his bicycle behind a stone wall in the shade of a sycamore tree.

It was not a good day for fishing, being hot with a hint of thunder in the air; he was glad to have completed the six miles to the stream. He untied his rod from the crossbar of his bike, pulled it out of the cloth sleeve and assembled the two sections. The rod was a fibreglass one measuring eight and a half feet, his first proper trout rod. He had hoped for a split cane like Grandpa's but the old man said he would have to wait a bit. Giles knew that only wealthy families like Wilberforce's at school, old generals, retired colonels, fishing doctors and senior gentlemen owned split canes – perhaps one day. . . . He was, in any case, proud of his rod which was a Christmas present. The reel and line had been purchased from a tackle shop where the man in charge had said he ought to have a net and fly box. His father, who did not fish, added these to the outfit.

The net had a wooden handle two feet long and arms which flicked up to extend the meshed bag: it was neither expensive nor foolproof as the meshes at times caught in the spreading arms and the whole would become jammed in a half-open position. The fly box was a heavy, black tin; beneath the single lid were compartments for the flies. Wilberforce at school had an expensive silver-coloured box of polished aluminium; the flies were enclosed in little compartments with individual transparent lids which sprang open at the touch of a finger. The box was flourished with some ostentation at the waterside.

Giles ran the line through the rings of the rod, the reel clicking sweetly as it unwound. He attached a 5X leader to the line and tied a small Blue Upright to the point. Picking up his tackle and bag, he walked down through the trees to the stream. It was a secluded water running off the moor and down through the woods, protected from the sun by a canopy of trees. Sunbeams cut slanting shafts through openings in the leaves to light patches of golden gravel. As he came closer to the water he moved with caution, making his final approach behind a bush through which he peered into the pool beyond. There were trout there but he could not see a really worthwhile fish. Six inches was the common size, eight would bring a craggy smile to Grandpa's face and could be taken to the kitchen. What he really wanted was a ten-inch fish – a specimen, as Wilberforce would say, a sizeable trout well above the six-inch limit. Wilberforce had landed a twelve-incher last term of which he had been justly proud and slightly condescending as he described the capture to his friend. He, Giles, must do as well, or better, and take a photograph to prove the truth of his account. He moved up the river until he came to an old sheep dip, long disused. A stone wall ran down his side of the stream, the other wall had collapsed into the water and now made hiding places for the trout. A wren had nested in one of the crevices in May; the moss, dried leaves and horsehair lining had been pulled out and were visible to Giles as he crept up on the likely secret place. The boy watched the moving water for a long time, just his head above the bank. As he peered the secrets of the rocks and currents were revealed and he saw The Specimen. The tail gave the fish away, for the whole of the trout looked almost black and the rocks behind were dark as well, but the tail was a little less black and it moved – very slightly. The Specimen had taken up a comfortable position in front of a rock where little swimming effort was required. He was large for the stream and there could be no doubt, as Wilberforce would say, drawing on his greater experience, that he would give a good account of himself. Giles stared; he was reluctant to do anything which might scare the fish, for there was satisfaction in just looking at the powerful shape. The trout would be experienced, he could not be otherwise, having lived for so long without falling victim to the heron or the otter. Any disturbance and he would disappear . . . . 'Pushed off. Too heavy a Woolworth's leader, I daresay', would be Wilberforce's comment: his leaders came from Farlow's of Pall Mall.

Giles backed down the bank, sat down and sought a solution. A Blue Upright would be no good – being insufficiently tempting. The bait had to be something succulent and surprising, a once-in-a-month delicacy which would be washed downstream if The Specimen did not take an immediate chance. At the same time it must not be something he had never seen before or he might be frightened. The mouthful must excite a memory of a satisfying experience. Giles did not use so many words in his mind but he would know what it was when he could think of it. Then the penny dropped. A frog, a small live frog was the answer, there could be no doubt. How could a frog possibly conceal deceit? Frogs were simple succulent creatures with wide and innocent eyes. Giles found a froglet in a swampy place close by which he had visited at Easter to collect tadpoles in a jar. The baby frogs were much the same size as his thumb nail and still had a small protruding tail. He picked one up and at once felt sorry for the creature. He had to think of a way to catch the trout and, at the same time, allow the froglet to escape. The capture of The Specimen could not be marred by the death of the bait.

From his fly box Giles took his largest fly, a No. 8 Peter Ross, which Grandpa said would catch a peal. He stripped the hook of all the dressing with his knife and tied it to the end of his leader. He picked up one of the baby frogs and held it in a dock leaf to keep it cool. Returning to the sheep dip the boy looked again with caution. The trout was still there, clearly watching out for food and not at all suspicious or disturbed. Giles crept away. Taking the froglet from the leaf, he slipped the hook through the very end of the tail, comforting himself with the thought that the last remnant of its tadpole life would fall off soon in any case and it would probably escape when its part in the plot had been completed.

He pushed his rod over the edge of the sheep dip wall with his right hand, let go the bait with his left; the frog swung over the stream, dropped into the water with a plop in front of The Specimen and set off strongly with a firm breast stroke for the far side. The Specimen, clearly astonished by this foolhardy behaviour, dropped back two feet, spun round once below the frantically swimming frog, and took it in a gulping swirl. The hook pierced his mouth which he hurriedly opened, the frog was ejected and, free once more, swam off. The Specimen fought hard, almost escaping when the arms of the net failed to click open but Giles found a sandy bay in which he beached the fish. He hit the trout on the head with part of a kitchen chair leg, his priest, gave it the 'coup-de-grace', or 'quietus', as Wilberforce would say. The thought of his friend reminded him of the photograph and other matters, such as weight and length, which would verify the truth of the tale he would tell on his return to school.

A breathless, hot and excited boy reached his grand-parent's house at tea-time. 'Grandpa, grandpa. Look, look. I've got a specimen, a beauty. Do you think it can be two pounds?' Grandpa looked, and a sadness and a happiness momentarily joined in his mind that such days for him were over. 'It really is a large one, perhaps a record for the stream. Where did you get him?' The story poured out in a spate of words, and the old man marvelled at the unchanged ways. Not that he would want to go through life again but, for a moment he had regrets and stifled a trace of envy as he took the photograph.

On the first day of term Giles ran into school clutching the picture. The carefully prepared description of the battle with the trout, to be delivered in matter-of-fact tones, stored ready in his mind. 'A two-pounder,' drawled the listening Wilberforce, 'not bad, not bad at all. By the way, take a look at this.' He produced an enlarged colour photograph of himself standing before an impressive Highland river: in his arms he held a salmon.

CHAPTER 6

AUGUST

A greater number of salmon were caught in August than any other month in the 14 rivers recorded by the South West Water Authority in 1985 and 1986. August 1984 was not so good and neither was 1987; owing to low rainfall for the month the summer run of grilse came in later in those two years, in September. A total of 18 rivers are recorded in the same area for sea trout. Catches for August in 1984 and 1985 were only

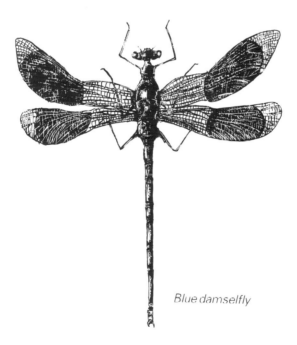

Blue damselfly

beaten by July; whilst the August 1986 total was the peak for that season.

Provided there is plenty of rain, August is a grand month for salmon and grilse. If there is little wet weather the chances are that river sea trout fishing at night will be rewarding in the settled conditions. You cannot have it both ways, wet for salmon and dry for peal, but the odds are that for migratory fish the month is kind to the angler. It may be that the sea trout are small in size, for now is the time of the little peal, the small Welsh sewin, and the Scottish finnock. The same goes for the salmon: grilse predominate in the 4–6 lb weight range. All the same, if you want action, the harvest and holiday month is hard to beat, particularly for sea trout. If salmon is your aim, it would be best to await the end of the month and September when there is usually more rain.

Now is the peak of the Scottish loch fishing for sea trout from drifting boats – the dapping rods will be out, scuttling bushy flies over the water surface. Surrounded by purple heather-clad hills above the silver-trunked birch trees at water level, one takes to the boats after a substantial breakfast of porridge, bacon and eggs, sausages and black pudding. Some anglers will go out from the highland hotels, others from lodges with fishing on their own water. Particulars of such houses for private parties of anglers may be obtained from a number of the leading estate and sporting agencies. Scottish solicitors are another likely source.

How will the trout man fare who stays at home in England? The heat and brightness of July fade gradually; the evenings start to draw in; the dusk rise of trout is earlier, allowing us to return home to bed at a civilized hour. Sedge fishing rewards us; the Invicta comes into its own, and a wet gale may enable us to take a memorable basket from the rolling waves of the wide, still waters. On the trout streams the Red Sedge and the Caperer catch those fish which swirl under the darkening green leaves of the oaks and the yellowing of the willow branches as the sun falls behind the hill. August can be a gentle, generous month – but I prefer her rough and wet.

To Loch Maree for sea trout

Amongst the earliest entries in my fishing diary are summer days in 1949 and 1950 at the Loch Maree Hotel in the north west of Scotland in August and September. Almost 40 years later a fishing friend, Dr Tom Owen, went to the same hotel between 13 and 18 July 1987. We subsequently compared notes on methods and results to reveal the pleasing knowledge that fish numbers have not fallen over the years. However, there are variables and Tom *is* a very good fisherman!

44 Looking up Loch Maree

Six September days between the 19th and the 24th in 1949 yielded 16 sea trout and finnock to my friend and myself. Amongst these were fish of 2½ lb, 4 lb and 5½ lb. Four came to the dap and 12 to wet flies fished off 11-ft split cane trout rods. The flies being, without exception, Black Pennel and Peter Ross – wet flies fished on 3X gut casts – whilst the Blue Zulu was on the dap. The total weight of fish was 25½ lb, an average of just over 1½ lb each. In fact, all the sea trout came in three days, the blank days being either flat calm or with a strong cold east wind.

There is little recorded information on the actual fishing, other than the comments that the three generous days were very bright with a moderate east wind and the following note, 'Fish long heavy line very deep. Trail bob over surface.' In 1949 the plastic-coated fly line was not yet in use. Dressed silk was the material and this sank unless greased. We did not grease those lines and so, when thoroughly soaked, the fish must have taken the flies well down. 'Fished long heavy line', must mean a long cast – there was probably time and distance for the flies to sink considerably as the boat drifted slowly down on the wind. Fishing deep is what one would expect in bright weather with an east wind; such conditions are not conducive to surface activity.

No doubt some sea trout followed the flies up to the top to take. 'Trail bob over surface' would be very effective with a long 11-ft fly rod – it being possible to start the trailing several yards from the boat. Heart stopping, those moments when a good sea trout comes for the bob! You must have the self-control not to strike, not to whip the fly away – let the trout go down, then tighten.

In mid-August 1950 with the same companion the six-day bag was 14 sea trout and finnock, totalling 21½ lb. The average weight was 1½ lb with a best fish of 4½ lb. Most of these trout came to the dap in a warm west wind. In other words they came up, whilst the previous year in the cold east wind they did not, being taken on a well-sunk wet fly.

*

Maree is a lovely mountain girt loch with enticing beats for the boats out from the hotel: Weedy Bay, North Shore, New Beat, Slattadale and Back of the Islands. Today some names are changed, but Ash is the best, being in direct line with the River Ewe. Isle of Maree only produced two finnock, totalling just over 2 lb for us on 16 August 1950 – no matter, the shingle beach is a lovely place to lunch. Tom told me that the dead tree-trunk is still there, pressed full of copper pennies green with age, offerings to the gods of chance by hopeful anglers. Not much has changed, but he cannot remember seeing the hulk of the beached launch which used to tow the boats to their beats. In the late 1940s outboard motors were in use.

How do Tom's catches in 1987 compare with ours of earlier years? On numbers in the boat he gave us a hiding. We averaged eight fish each in 1949 and seven in 1950. Tom took 17 to his own rod, five were 'good ones' and 'about a dozen finnock'. Twice as many as ourselves, and substantial fish they were: 4½, 2½, 3, 2½, 2 and 1½ lb – and he lost a large one at the net. One remembers lost fish: they are always larger than the others! According to Tom the end of July is one of the best times, and the best moments seemed to come just before packing up for the day. Certainly the afternoon was more productive than the morning.

He took his fish on the dap, for which the hotel loaned him a long rod and Terylene floss blow line; to this he tied 1 yard of 10-lb nylon for the fly. Of the various flies he tried, Loch Ordie, Blue Zulu, Fore and After, a Black-Pennel-type of buzzy lure was the most killing pattern. 'What did you do with the fish?', I asked.

'Well, I ate quite a few of the finnock for breakfast, froze the rest whole, without cleaning, and brought them home.' They must have been good, for he admitted that he ate the lot within a few weeks.

I cannot remember a salmon being caught on my visits, although we saw one leap. In addition, a fish of 13 lb was brought in by one of the boats to the hotel where there was unresolved controversy on the salmon/sea trout identification. It seems that the dap is used more today than 40 years ago, but no doubt it is still wise to take a fly rod, a long one, suitable for the boat, as a change from dapping and in case one sees a salmon.

As always, there is more to fishing than catching fish. Tom has a discerning palate; he admits to frying his finnock in butter. Can you imagine anything more delightful? As he observed when fishing the Taw from a north Devon pub, 'They gave me a jolly good breakfast, sausages, eggs, bacon, kidneys, that sort of thing, fried bread too, and a first class dinner. If they do that I find I can manage in between.'

*

The requirements for sea trout dapping are simple: a long rod of 17 or 18 ft, a reel with 100 yards of monofilament backing and twenty yards of Terylene floss blow line. To the end of the blow line, attach one yard of 10-lb nylon and the dapping fly. The great thing about the fly is that it is a bumbly creation – plenty of palmered hackle wound from the bend to the eye of a No. 8 or No. 10 hook. Three black cock hackles would make a good mouthful, particularly if the body is ribbed with fine gold or silver tinsel. Waterproof several flies in Supafloat (available in Britain and America) before going out. A stock of flies prepared in advance saves time on the water, for they become soggy after an hour or two, and particularly after being battered by a fish.

Without doubt the greatest contribution to the success of the day is made by the boatman. It is he who knows the best places, the shallow banks, and the most productive drifts. All the angler has to do is keep the blow line billowing out in the wind, and the fly scuttering over the surface of the loch without the nylon touching the water. One thing more is required of the man with the rod – an iron control when a fish comes up that freezes all action until the sea trout has submerged with the fly. Tighten when the tail waves goodbye.

Young fly fishers – morning, evening, and the night

4 August 1983. River Lyd in morning. 4 small brown trout on Kite's. A good evening and until 1.00 am on Dart. With Nigel, Ian, Simon and Eric. A number of small brownies and then 4 sea trout on Black Lure or Black Chenille. 11 oz, 1 lb, 1 lb and a large one of 3 lb 12 oz.

On summer holiday junior fly fishing courses we have a carefully programmed day when sea trout are to be taken in that night, a schedule which is undemanding during the morning and the afternoon. Energy has to be conserved. Something must be left for the dark hours. Breakfast is over by 9.00 am, to be followed by kitting out for fishing on our little trout stream, the Lyd, which runs below the house. We met up that day at 9.15 am in the rod room where, after a short discussion on upstream dry fly technique I issued each of the boys with a 7- or 8-ft rod, a 5X knotless tapered leader and half a dozen dry flies. Those flies, how each boy looks at them with hope: Wickham, Sedge, Kite's, and some from the inner fastnesses of their own boxes. What treasured hoards those boxes store. Valued but often useless through age and use. Soft-hackled, beaten-up specimens.

The outfits are made up, the leaders greased to within a yard of the fly, which is waterproofed by immersion in the floatant bottle, then off we trudge in thigh boots – down over the fields to the Lyd.

45 *Four sea trout to four boys. Dart* (4 August 1983)

46 *A boy removes the hook from a small peal*

47 *For safety boys fish at night in pairs*

The water is low in August, but there are unsuspected deep holes under the roots of trees which have been cut out by the current in the winter floods; the trout are in these holes. It takes time to discover where to look; where to cast the fly; where to plop the upstream nymph. When these secrets have been revealed, and the depths plumbed with a copper-bodied nymph, trout start to be plucked from these hiding holes to fight, every yard of the way, until beached on a sandy bank. 'What shall we do with the catch Mr Bingham?' The expectant ones always ask me this before we make a start. 'Anything over ½ lb you can have for breakfast. Six-ouncers go to Jinx the cat. Lesser ones go back after being released under water with artery forceps. If you would like a fried trout for breakfast we'll clean them in the river with my pocket knife.' At noon I leave them to think things out for themselves. An hour or two later they trail into the rod room with the catch: one trout of 10 or 12 oz if we are lucky; two 6-ouncers for the cat; a number of tales of doubtful veracity of the ones which broke them around a root and escaped in a flurry of foam.

They are encouraged to sleep in the afternoon because, going after sea trout in the coming night, they will not be in bed until the early hours. Some do drop off. Others, the older ones of 15 years, tie a lure or two for the coming night. The peal flies they dress are simple: black, blue and silver; slim killing patterns with finger-pricking hooks. Having tied them, these flies have a magic power in their imagination. Each boy is developing an eagerness, an involvement, an understanding when he ties his own flies and then catches a peal on one in the dark. The size of the peal does not matter; it is the 'take' which counts. The moment when the rod bends, the line lifts and straightens and he is proved right. That is the moment. When he has caught one on a previous night he has faith; he can see it all come true again as he winds the silk around the hook during the siesta hour.

Tea in the rod room at 5.00 pm, followed by the selection of larger rods for the night ahead. 'When we reach the Dart at 7.00 pm we'll fish downstream wet with small flies for wild browns for an hour, then put on sea trout leaders and lures whilst the light holds before a picnic supper.' There is an issue of No. 14 Greenwell's Glory wet flies for the trout fishing, and a replacement 5X leader to those whose nylon did not withstand the rigours of the morning. Each boy is then supplied with two 9-ft leaders tapered to a 9-lb point, together with two No. 8 Black Lures and a 1-in. Alexandra tube fly; these are for the peal. A torch and a landing net are issued to each. The equipment and game bag, which holds food, drink, and spare dry clothes, are put into the car. Off we go across Dartmoor to the lower river, closer to the sea from which the sea trout come. We see ponies and sheep, ravens and buzzards, rooks, jackdaws and a curlew picking and probing for sustenance from the heather, the grass and the green mosses of the swampy areas.

At the river we startle a cormorant which has flown up the valley from the estuary and sits on a boulder, replete and satisfied after fishing for sea trout in the river pools. We frighten him, and the great black bird lumbers away in a slow ungainly feet-splashing take-off, then circles in the air before heading

Rabbit

down river, neck outstretched for the sea. From 7.00 pm until 9.00 pm we fish the little wet Greenwells. Casting down and across the tiny yellow-bodied fly flickers and twists its way across the stickles, rising and falling with the swirls of the current. Sometimes a pluck twitches up the line to feeling fingers as a trout rises in curiosity to test this thing which can swim and hold a position against the flow of the current. At times a salmon parr takes hold – now is the justification for fishing with a barbless hook. Barbless or not he is soon set free with a twitch of the forceps on the hook shank. As evening comes trout rise in the eddies and under the banks, going for the sedges which rise and fall at the water's edge, and the clouds of midges which drift up the river on the south west wind.

We meet again at 9.00 pm to change to sea trout leaders and flies whilst there is light to see to tie the knots. Someone has a 12-oz trout, another has seen two peal leap in the pool below the rookery, and there are accounts of salmon showing further down the river. For a time chatter ceases as mouths are filled with food, squash is drunk and a little coffee, saving two flasks for a hot drink later in the night. Sea trout are jumping in front of us, and excitement rises as a large one lifts out of the water by the land drain to send waves across the pool.

The four boys go to allotted places to fish in pairs, for company and assistance in the netting. One couple stays at the picnic site which is our base camp for the night – the site is at the head of a productive piece of water. I take the other couple to the tail of the lowest pool and there we await the night. One rod will be used between us, and this is set down by the river's edge with the leader, already cleaned with 'sink mix', soaking in the water. 'Now,' I say, 'I'll start you off, then when you see the form you carry on by yourselves.' Several peal have jumped, and there is an expectancy amongst us. 'If you hook a peal keep your rod up, let him run if he wishes, drop the rod point if he leaps close by. When he's tired he'll turn on his side, showing a silver side –then's the time to net him out. Don't scoop about with the net until he's played out and visible on the surface.' After ten minutes I leave them, handing over a CB radio. 'I'll call you up on the hour. Channel 30. Be listening.'

I move away to leave them engrossed, enveloped by the night. Upriver one boy has landed a peal, a bright 1-lb fish. The other has the rod and is casting with determination into the darkness under the trees lining the far bank. 'There are peal there Mr Bingham. We've seen several and one gave me a pull.' I direct him to cast to the tail of the pool, to the final two or three yards before the black silent sliding water breaks into the stickle and runs off gurgling. There is no response from the fish. 'What have you got on?'

'A Black Chenille,' he replies. 'One I tied this afternoon.' He pulls the line in through the rings and shows me. The fly is rather fat in the head. This often happens when starting to tie flies – one bunches up too much material at the head and takes too many turns of silk in the whipping. 'Come out, and we'll have a change.' He backs out of the water and we crouch in the field, away from the river, a pool of torchlight illuminating three faces as he takes one of my slim Black Lures. The nylon is threaded through the eye of the hook and tied on with a Turle knot whilst insects zoom in on the light. Then, after a quick wipe to the leader with the sink mix, he tries again in the same place. It is 11.45 pm when his rod arches into a fighting curve as a peal takes the fly. In due course the 1-lb peal is netted by the other boy who stumbles a little as he backs out onto the bank. We thump the fish on the head and wrap it in a polythene bag as protection from the slugs which always come out of the grass at night and will feed on your fish if they can.

The score at our end is two by midnight. 'Call up the others on the CB. See if they've had any luck.' We pull out the aerial, tune in and the radio crackles as a stranger asks another stranger for his position. Perhaps there is a Royal Marine exercise on the moor. We establish contact with the boys amidst crackles, voices and other interference, then switch to clearer air on channel 14. 'Any luck?' They have one small one and say that all has gone quiet. 'Come up here. We'll have some coffee, then go on for another hour.'

Ten minutes later the pinpricks of torchlight are visible as they wend their way upstream. We eat, and drink coffee, and admire the three small peal. It is not really dark, although it is the middle of the night. Behind the clouds there is a moon, which we cannot see, but she lights the clouds from above, and they, in turn, diffuse her light, shedding a pale glow over the earth. We are alone in the dark, a protecting envelope, comforting in its presence and cloudy warmth. 'Come on. Let's have a final go by the pipe. I'll wade out and you all follow, in line, hands on the shoulder of the man in front. No stumbling. I'll cast. You play anything we hook [this to Simon]. I'll net.'

The cork rod butt is firm in my hand; the reel clicks softly as it gives up line; backwards and forwards goes the rod in the air, lengthening the line which shoots forward to pitch the fly under the far bank where the peal lie. All is still. An owl hoots behind us from an ivy-covered trunk in Rookery Wood, a dark mass of trees on the hill which slopes down to the river. The down and across casts have brought no response. We switch to upstream throws, retrieving line faster than the current drifts the fly downstream. Below the chalk-coloured shadow of cow parsley heads on the far bank we have a savage take. There is a momentary churning of water, I wind up the slack line onto the reel and hand the rod to Simon. The peal takes off upstream, effortlessly stripping out the yards. The boys watch, eyes straining – 'There he is'. A leap and crash – almost invisible at 20 yards. Silence follows but for the clicking of the reel as Simon takes in slack line. Contact is regained as the peal turns and makes for the far bank, running down the edge, looking for a hole, a snag, relief from the invisible pressure of the line and leader. Rod held high, Simon controls and subdues him. There is a wallowing, a splash, a dark snake-like movement on the surface and the dull gleam of a fish under which I slide the net and lift him out.

We all regain the bank and bring an end with the priest. He was a fine fish, that peal of 3 lb 12 oz. We gather around and admire the powerful shape, the square end to the tail, the hunched shoulder. 'Come on. Time to pack up.' Anything else would be an anticlimax. Back across Dartmoor in the car they sleep in slumped oblivion, unaware of the sheep lying, chewing, on the warm tarmac of the road; the owl in the car lights; the rabbits running before us, terrified and aimless.

River level rise stimulates salmon

25 August 1979. Dart. 12.15 pm. Lost a bright fish of about 7 lb on a double No. 6 Thunder & Lightning in run above Saucepan; jumped and came unstuck after five minutes.
1.00 pm top of Iron Bars. 6 lb.
4.00 pm run above the Saucepan. 8 lb. Went down through Saucepan. I got into river and followed. Netted out in weir.
5.00 pm under sycamore below Rock Hole. 5 lb.
All on a No. 8 trebled 1¼ in. Copper Dart tube fly.
River on the low side; rose 1 in. A soft day with plenty of midges.

Without looking at a calendar I know that 25 August 1979 was a Saturday on which a junior course ended after breakfast, the boys having fished for the previous four days. This left me free to go to the river where Tony Allen lent me a pair of gum boots; in my hurry to be fishing I had left my own waders at home. Tony then departed to his house in Hampshire to fish on the Test that evening – minus his boots.

On my own I walked down to the water. In the river my water-level marker rock for that place was barely submerged. By this I mean it was covered by water to the depth of the first joint in my index finger. One finger joint is a low level, indicating that fish are unlikely to be found other than in the necks of the pools or other deep channels. If the rock is not submerged it is barely worth fishing the fly – the salmon will have relapsed into a torpor to await the next spate. A hand's breadth of water over the rock tells that almost all the water will be fishable, but if the rock is submerged to the depth of a forearm one will only have a chance in the wide tails of the pools. On 25 August there was a finger joint of water, a 'just possible' level. As to the weather, it was what the Irish call a 'soft day' – witnessed by the midges and the little lumps they raised on my wrists, ears and neck. A soft day is a day of hope. Damp, mizzly, cloudy, and boggy underfoot from a little overnight rain – a sunbather's nightmare and a salmon fisher's delight. But the water? Barely enough.

The first fish came unstuck, as I recorded. It jumped and away came the double hook. We all lose fish at times, but a double is never as good as a treble because it only has two hooks instead of three and in most cases a longer shank, which may lever out the hook hold. That fish came off, and my heart sank at the loss of what might turn out to be the only customer. The diary, unwittingly, now discloses a change in the river condition between noon and 1.00 pm: it rose. Not much, but it must have come up. How is that apparent to me when the events happened so many years ago and I was, at the time of taking those fish, half a mile from the marker rock? A No. 6 Thunder & Lightning on the Dart is a fly used in low water, but the fly used 45 minutes later for the 1.00 pm fish was a 1¼-in. Copper Dart which is ¼ in. longer than the normal 1-in. low water model. A size of 1¼ in. indicates with certainty that there had been a river rise, and probably a little extra colour came down as well – there had been an hour or two of rain in the night, and the slight water bulge from the catchment now reached my area.

The second salmon, the 8-pounder, came from the lie where the first had been lost, which illustrates the fact that a good lie is worth fishing several times in a day, in suitable water levels, even when it has already yielded a salmon or two. Fish move up the river by day as well as at night in a small spate, new occupants arrive, and there may have been more than one fish in residence in the first place. Of course, the 8-pounder could have been the fish lost in the morning, but this is doubtful. A salmon will sometimes come again after an hour or two if only lightly pricked, but the chances of a second go at the fly after a five-minute tussle are unlikely. This salmon went down through Saucepan; I got into river to follow it, and then netted it out in the weir. There is nowhere to net a fish in the run above the Saucepan. No slack water, no small bay, no sandy beach is available for beaching. As one is unable to go upriver in that place it is as well to encourage them to go down. This course means a watery journey for the angler, who has to cover the 100 yards to the weir, sometimes in, and sometimes out, of the river. Remember to remove any valuables from your pocket. The third fish, a 5-lb grilse, was further down the river, closer to the car. He must have given little trouble, for I don't remember him, but the lie under the sycamore tree is a killing spot if the river is at a reasonable height.

On such a day in a familiar water one is aware of a change in the river level by the speed and colour of the flow. Leaves drift by in season; other flotsam and white bubbles bounce upon the ripples. I suspected that the river had risen during the time I had been fishing and this was confirmed by the marker rock on the way home – it was submerged by two finger joints!

*

We all know that water levels in salmon fishing are crucial to success on those rivers which are not spring-fed, and even in those a little extra helps. A spell of continuous rain in a spate river catchment area after a week or two of dry weather will cause a rise in the river level for a period of time whilst a bulge of water runs down the valley. The moment this bulge reaches the place where you are fishing is a great time for a salmon, for 15 or 20 minutes before the flow becomes too full and dirty. During the full flow it is just possible to catch running fish as they rest in the wide tail of a pool where it shallows out above a rapid they have just negotiated. When the rain ceases the river may rise for a while before the fall begins: the gradual reduction which follows is the longest and usually most productive period for taking fish. This series of events is common knowledge, and you should think yourself lucky if the whole chain took place during a week's fishing holiday.

Above this desirable plane is the golden day, a rarity, rich in rewards and beyond our reasonable expectations. It is a day when the water is already fishable; new salmon have arrived, are no longer running, and just settling. Then, before they become too calm and lose the edge of their spate excitement, a *little* more flow stirs them up. You now have a river which is falling, then rising, then falling between very narrow limits, and in that order. This keeps the fish on edge; they are alert; they don't know whether to run or whether to stay. An undecided fish can be rash and take the fly with aggression. There is the well-known story of the angler who set his gillie to throw rocks into a pool before he fished it down, on the theory that this unsettled the salmon. It is unwise to deride such innovative actions – you never know with salmon.

Salmon and grilse in unsettled water

24 August 1985. Dart. High water. Lara caught a 5-lb grilse in the morning in Hill Pool on a 1½-in. Black Dart tube fly. I had a fish of 13 lb, very fresh in Dark Pool.

When we reached the river after breakfast it was almost too high after the night's rain, but if you have driven some way to fish you might as well chance your arm. In any case, as the rain had stopped, it was only a matter of time

48 *5-lb grilse and 13-lb salmon on 1½-in. Black Dart tube fly* (24 August 1985)

before a fall commenced. I tackled up for Lara. She had a 12-ft carbon fibre rod, St John reel and a light-green floating line. We tied a 1½-in. Black Dart to the end of a 9-ft leader of 17-lb nylon, and off she went. I said I would follow with the net when my own outfit was made up. We usually fish together with one net but two patterns of fly – perhaps Black Dart and Hairy Mary, or Black Dart and Copper Dart or possibly, in lowish water, a double Thunder & Lightning. It all depends upon the feeling one has for the conditions. Lara usually opens for us by fishing down each pool, and then I follow with the alternative fly. We keep in sight of each other. My weapon that day was a 12-ft ferruled Sharpe's impregnated split cane with a wide spooled 3¾-in. Hardy Perfect reel. My favourite salmon fly outfit on a small river is the 12-ft spliced Sharpe – I do not know why it was not with me on that day.

Hill Pool is only fishable in high water. As the level drops the fish depart, running on upstream to rocky holes and deep hiding places. They don't hang about for long in Hill Pool. There must have been 75 yd between us when Lara gave a shout, then stood quite still looking mystified:

A fish Dad. It came into that gravel bay where I had brought the fly before lifting off into the back cast. It picked up the fly as it brushed across the sand, then spat it out and swam off. I couldn't do anything – there was no room to move the fly further, and I was too surprised to set the hook.

This was a remarkable event, for it was possible to see that the salmon had followed the fly into water less than 2 ft deep. 'Fish down on him again. Start back up there.' Lara moved up-river for 25 yd and repeated her actions. This time the fish, the 5-lb grilse, took just outside the bay where, after she had played him out, he was netted in this little backwater.

We fished on down for three or four hours during which time it rained and the river started to lift again – very slightly. We both covered Dark Pool twice. Nothing stirred in the river. Not a fin showed, we were wet and becoming depressed. Lara's soaked blonde hair hung down over the shoulders of her waxed jacket, and my cap was sodden. Cold and hungry, with white hands, she went back to the car. I decided to fish once more over Dark Pool. This I did without result, hooked up the fly on the reel mount and was just walking away when there was a splosh behind me. Sploshes always make one whirl about and there, in the pool tail, were the settling waves of the disturbed water. Fish often jump when they enter a pool and clearly this chap had just forced his way up the rapids, entered the quieter water and leaped. Fish which mark their entrance by a leap are usually takers! This show is followed by a reconnoitre of the area, a swim around the pool, and then a position is taken up in a lie which is comfortable at the prevailing water height. In this case, the lie was in the middle of the pool, there being insufficient water, by two or three inches, to cover the tail to a depth satisfactory to a salmon. Fish like about 4 ft of water if they are to lie in the run-off of Dark Pool, and as it wasn't quite there, he would move up to the middle. I dropped the fly under the far bank, turned the rod tip upstream and swung the fly in a fast sweeping curve over the lie which, surely, held that fish. He didn't waste time, but came up in a broad-flanked taking turn and went down with the tube treble firmly in the scissors.

Now, I thought, I'll just let you settle a little, remove some of your steam with five minutes of steady pressure and then, when you are a trifle out of breath, stir you up for the finale. Not a bit of it. That fish was an individualist. No rules were made for him. Without waiting for me, swinging like a demented gibbon around a tree trunk at the very extremity of the bank, he set off for the next pool up the river. In and out of the tree roots he went. No sooner was one snag negotiated than he found another – then turned about and went hard for the sea. Whether he was subjected to strain or given slack he remained unimpressed and continued to do his own thing. For a time it seemed he might be foul-hooked, so uncontrollable were his flights. In the end, he found a deep gulley under my feet. He was, literally, below my boots. There he took up residence. The rod butt now pointed to the far bank, the centre section curved over and the tip pointed back and down into the gulley under my feet. It couldn't go on of course, and in the end he was mine, but it is not often a 13-lb salmon takes half-an-hour to land.

Do sea trout feed in fresh water?

Two years ago my answer to this question would have been, 'At times they take a natural fly, but they do not *feed* to the extent that body weight will be gained.' With salmon one could give a categorical 'No' to the question, and then someone would say, 'I once saw a salmon on the Hampshire Avon taking mayfly. It came up to my Wulff, and when landed its mouth was crammed with the natural.' Clearly, as always in fishing, one cannot give absolute answers. With sea trout, two years ago, I would have come down on the side of the non-feeders. This is still my view for the majority – but not for a small minority of peal, particularly small ones. More sea trout may feed in fresh water than we imagine. If it is accepted that fly fishing is a highly inefficient method of taking migratory game fish, perhaps only one in ten being interested in our lures, then, of that tenth, quite a high proportion may feed intermittently. After all, sea trout take a dapped fly, and also a dry fly at times. These are insect imitators, even if as a general, rather than an accurate, representation. Salmon do not take these floaters in this country, at least, not often.

13 August. Dart. 3 small peal, all about 1 lb. No. 8 Black Lure, tandem Black Lure and Silver Stoat's Tail. Bryan O'Neill and myself. Fine warm night. Three-quarter moon. Caught 1 in the mist which came up. Unusually, 1 of the peal had a full stomach: stonefly creepers, some nymphs and a wasp.

and:

49 *Bryan O'Neill with three small peal. Dart* (13 August 1987)

50 *It is wise to knock a peal on the head whilst still in, or over, the net*

51 Even a 1-lb peal may be marked by the nets at sea

18 August 1987. Dart. 3 peal. 2 lb 14 oz. Black Lure and 1-in. Alex tube. 2 fish empty. 1 stuffed with stonefly creepers, midge pupae and a black beetle.

One never knows what the autopsy will reveal. This gives hope to those dedicated people who tackle river sea trout by day: not a particularly rewarding occupation! Success can come in daylight with stealth, a very fine leader, a single peal lying by itself and a bit of luck. A single peal is more stalkable – in a shoal many pairs of eyes are on the alert. Success may also come if there is a spate, some of the largest peal are taken whilst salmon fishing.

On the whole, I am sure that sea trout do not feed, as brown trout, in a predictable manner with a noticeable rise at certain times of the day. At the same time, it is clear from these two diary entries that a few small peal feed purposefully at night. No doubt this coincides with those periods of activity after dusk and before dawn when you are most likely to take a fish or two.

Lemon Gray, author of *Torridge Fishery*, clearly considered that peal feed during *some* nights. He wrote in one section of his book: 'When really on the feed, from dusk onwards . . .', and, 'On nights when they don't intend to feed seriously . . .'.

Two salmon from the Tamar

My telephone rang on the evening of 18 August 1985. The caller, Bob, a former fishing pupil, was at first hard to understand owing to the excitement in his voice at catching his first two salmon. A little Scottish wine may also have had something to do with his slight incoherence. He is a valued neighbour, by which I mean in our sparsely populated region that he lives ten miles away on the other side of the Tamar. Today he is a fishing partner with no small measure of skill and a large ration of endurance as he follows the river bank. When fishing together, I am in awe of his total disregard for physical discomfort and wet feet, despite his superior status as a senior citizen. Bob kindly complied with my request for an account of the manner in which his salmon duck was broken. In his own words here is a truthful fisherman's tale.

*

'On Sunday 18 August 1985 in the afternoon I was fishing with Michael Beecham on the Cornish and tidal side of the weir at Gunnislake on the Tamar. The tide was on its way up the river and, as ever, I was hoping this would be the day I caught my first salmon. That had been my hope on all the other days when I had been lucky enough to have a rod on this famous river, as a very bright-green learner in my first season of owning my own tackle.

'The beat I was on consists of the weir itself and the two fish passes, only one

52 *The Duke of Bedford's dairy at Endsleigh on the Tamar. In the nineteenth century this was used as a salmon larder*

53 *It helps to know the diet of a trout. This dead fish is being 'spooned' to examine the stomach contents*

54 *Boys by the dam at Fernworthy*

55 Removing a hook from a trout

56 The Invicta is a great fly for autumn trout

of which can be fished from our bank, the pool below and the run out of it over a small sill, and another pool down to a final weir. The main weir at the top of the beat marks the limit of the tidal water.

'The river was in good order, there having been enough rain to give a spate but not so much as to colour the water. It rained on and off during the day. Michael, my host, put me in the weir pool to spin. I was using my Farlow's Farlight 9-ft spinning rod with a Mitchell 300A fixed spool reel loaded with 18.7-lb Platil monofilament. The business end of the outfit was an 18-in. trace of 15-lb Platil, a ¾-oz Wye lead and a No. 2 Red & Black Mepps spoon. There is a strong flow over the weir making a ¾-oz weight necessary to keep down the Mepps. I was casting directly downstream of the fish pass.

'At about 3.00 pm, whilst reeling in, I thought for a moment that the bait had snagged on the underwater gravel bank which has formed below the fish pass on my side. However, I knew I was wrong when my first salmon jumped as the hook took hold. After that, everything became blurred as I tried to remember all I had been told about playing a fish: rod tip down when it jumps; don't wind in when its pulling; pump up the rod and wind if the fish becomes morose; brake on when you can and off if the salmon heads for the sea. Out of the corner of my eye, I could see Herbie Symons, doyen of river wardens, but now retired, anxiously watching from downstream, and Michael hurrying up with his Gye net. I persuaded the fish into the back eddy but it then dived into the flume of the fish pass. The fight continued. After ten minutes there came a slackening of effort in the fish's runs and I saw the silver glint of the belly again and again. Michael did a neat job with the net and I had caught my first salmon – a clean fish of 12½ lb. After a stiff tot all round, and a photograph, Michael said "You'd better go and catch another one." I did! A 12-lb fish came an hour later in the same place on the same bait. This time I was more controlled and I managed to do most of the right things at the right time.'

CHAPTER 7

SEPTEMBER

In the early 1940s, Llyn Llygeirian on Anglesey in North Wales held a fine stock of brown trout. They were not tiddlers those fish, for on the thwart of the boat from which we fished the lake Mr Mounfield, the owner, had chiselled two grooves. The trout we caught were laid flat on the wood between these marks, which were at least 12, and probably 14 in. apart. As a teenager in September I bicycled from a holiday home at Trearddur Bay over Four Mile Bridge, then due north to the lake, a distance of 12 miles. The journey, which seemed mostly uphill, was undertaken because Mounfield had said, after a fishless August day, 'The fishing improves, they come on again, in September.' He knew his lake and he was right. His remark is applicable to many trout fisheries, both running and still waters.

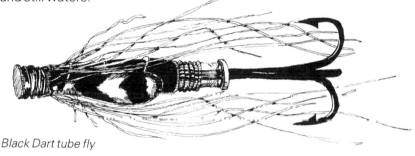

Black Dart tube fly

Trout no longer have to seek the cool depths of lakes, for the surface areas are at a comfortable temperature and there they will feed on a variety of insect life throughout the middle of the day. It is no longer necessary to fish the early or late hours, in fact both of these times may now be too chill for sport. Ten o'clock in the morning until tea-time will be the main period in which to hook and net your trout. Some of the brownies, both wild and stocked, will be taking on spawning hues. Some should be released to fulfil their life cycle; especially those clearly full of eggs or milt. Such trout are not worth eating. Rainbows, the non-breeding triploids, will be in fine condition.

All through the spring and summer the salmon population has been building in the rivers which are heavily stocked by now with grilse, summer fish, and rather stale springers. To the angler, September is one of the most prolific salmon months, and there is no need to spin, for the fish will come up with alacrity to a fly fished off a floating line. Those wishing to flick out a spoon bait, from a fixed spool reel, find the salmon will also come up to the golden whirr of metal if you chuck upstream and spin back fast. As with wild brown trout, salmon also have gravid hens amongst their numbers: such fish should be returned. Single-hooked flies are fished by some in September, enabling an easy release of over-ripe hens.

Most salmon will now be in the headwaters of the rivers, closing with the spawning beds, but newcomers on this breeding race are still entering the estuaries and may be caught in the lower reaches of the fresh waters. Indeed, on some rivers, the main run of the whole season does not come in from the sea until the autumn and early winter.

Sea trout are past their peak, which was in July and August. Peal, sewin, finnock, call them as local custom dictates, are becoming dark in colour. Not only have they lost their silver flanks but the flesh has softened. September peal may not be worth eating unless caught close to the sea. Good fishing at night may be experienced up to about the 10th of the month, but thereafter the nights grow dark and chill. When there is no moon this darkness brings no enclosing comfort, it is too black, in contrast to warm lights beckoning behind you from the windows of your home upon the hill.

Four boys, two trout, one grilse

4 September 1985. Dart. Jonathan, Ned, Toby and Henry. 2 brown trout. One 5-lb grilse on 1-in. Copper Dart in stickle above Stoney Pool. Very wet day.

The river is a 45-minute run by car from the house and, being a spate river, the journey is always something of a gamble in that the water level can only roughly be predicted before leaving home. An inverted dustbin lid is a helpful rain gauge, but the rainfall at my house is about 47 in. per annum compared with 79 in. at Princetown and 55 in. in the area of our beat near Buckfastleigh. It could be raining on Dartmoor whilst dry at home. The estimation of the river level from this distance is further complicated by the time the rain will take to run down the valley and whether the rain is light or heavy. It is all something of a gamble, and the only thing to do is to go and have a look; equip yourself with both trout and salmon tackle to cover all eventualities.

57 *The four boys and the 5-lb grilse* (4 September 1985)

58 *Sam Cadman with a 6 lb 10-oz rainbow taken by his father on a No. 12 Pheasant Tail Nymph*

On 4 September a course of four boys, all friends and all between 9 and 11 years old, were staying in the fisherman's wing of our house. As this was their second day they had already covered the basics of trout casting, learned two knots and a little about wet fly fishing for trout on a still water. Because it was raining in the early morning there was a fair chance that the river would start to rise by tea-time that afternoon to give us a chance at a grilse. We therefore made the decision that they should have a day at downstream wet fly for trout on the Dart, whilst we also took one salmon fly rod and net on the chance that the rain would continue and the river start to rise. We thus set off with four trout rods of between 7 ft 6 in. and 8 ft 6 in. in accordance with the physical capacity of the boys, a supply of 5X leaders and many small wet flies.

We arrived at the river in the middle of the morning after a drive across the moor where it rained lightly but steadily – there would be a chance at the grilse later in the day if the water rose before colouring. It was a grand fishing morning: cloudy, warm, breezy and wet. In addition, the water was clear for the trout, although too low for salmon. We tackled up the trout rods, wiped down the nylon leaders with sink mix and cast out – down and across. Stoney Pool is wide, calm and deep; it holds a stock of good trout, and I have myself taken a brown of 2¾ lb there at night whilst peal fishing. Trout were rising, many trout, but rather far from the bank for the boys to reach. Backwards and forwards went the rods, out sailed the little flies, tangles formed in leaders, hook points broke on stones, boots filled with water as the boys went in too far. Such matters are in the normal order of events for a 10-year-old. Sometimes a trout took hold, was beached and released, for boys do not carry trout nets on the Dart where they are often put down and forgotten, or fall off their trouser-belts unnoticed and are lost. I tried a Red Sedge, casting out into the middle of the pool where the trout were cruising and feeding, one behind the other, and the little fly attracted them. As soon as one was hooked, I thrust the rod into the hands of the nearest boy, who drew in the line over his rod hand forefinger, reeled up and beached the trout. They are always taught to recover line onto the reel when playing a trout –this may not be essential on a still water where the fish is played from a static position, but it is unwise to allow coils of line to form around one's feet as a habit. If the line is not recovered onto the reel when salmon fishing, but allowed to fall upon the bank, sooner or later it will snag upon a stick or your boot and then, if the salmon swims fast down river, a break is possible when the line cannot run free.

Before lunch two of the boys came upriver to a stickle just above the pool. In the tail of this rough water is a flat calm place with a surface area of not more than 2 or 3 square yards. Underneath the flat area is a hole about 4 ft deep at low water where grilse rest from time to time. The water had not yet started to rise, but even so a fish turned beneath the fly, showing us a fleeting glimpse of a curved white side. We left him to settle, deciding to try the salmon again later in the day at the exact moment when the river began to rise.

We had lunch in the rain, eating damp sandwiches, drinking hot coffee from the flasks, and shaking the water out of sodden tweed caps. In the afternoon I watched the river level constantly, for a rise would come, of that there was no doubt. It would come suddenly and allow 20 minutes fishing; then our chance would be lost in the thickening, deepening flow. It never ceases to amaze me that a 1-in. rise in the river at the beginning of a spate, over a lie 50 or 60 in. deep, will trigger a salmon to take. But it does have a stimulating effect on the fish, and it did excite that grilse to take the 1-in. Copper Dart. The water was low, and the 1-in. fly is our low water model, particularly when some of the bucktail is plucked out to make a skimpy specimen. Well, up he came, down he went, the rod was raised and Jonathan helped me to battle it out in the rain. The fish went down river, over shallow places, between rocks and through runs. We followed as best we could, sliding, slipping, soaking and, in my case, sometimes swearing. At last he was netted, knocked on the head and we all stood around to admire the slimness of his streamlined beauty.

It is always worth trying a lie for a second fish, but by the time we had sorted out the tackle, and ourselves, the water was rising fast and any companion with whom he may have shared the lie had probably moved away. We called it a day and went home, walking across the fields in squelching boots.

The Invicta

11 September 1987. Fernworthy reservoir on Dartmoor. 9 brown trout. Total 10 lb 9 oz. Best 1 lb 7 oz. Fly – Invicta. In a heavy south west wet gale blowing into the north corner of the dam. First experience of fly fishing for Ken who took 2 trout, and Mike who landed 4. Myself 3. We fished from 2.00 pm until 5.00 pm after a morning of instruction.

The Invicta wet fly is a cross between a sedge fly imitator and a visually attracting lure – one has it both ways. The sedge season is a long one, spreading over the months from June to September and even into October, and that does not include the Grannom which hatches in April but, in my experience, is not of marked interest to the trout. This wet fly is intended to represent a hatching sedge: that moment when the fly leaves its protecting larval case at the water surface. The wings of the natural fly slope back over the body; also in the hen pheasant wings of the Invicta. The living fly has two antennae and these, with legs, are represented by the springy yellow-dyed seal's fur of the body, which should be ribbed with gold tinsel. Thus we have, in addition to the immitative aspect, the two main requirements of a successful lure: a striped body in a colour at the red end of the spectrum – yellow.

The most successful manner of fishing this fly is as a dropper on a 9-ft leader. If a dropper of 3 in. is positioned 3 ft below the line/leader junction the fly may be trickled over the water surface in the final yards of the retrieve. Fished in this manner the trout come up from below to take with a wallop – before the sedge escapes in the air!

The 11 September was wet, rough, but not cold. The Invicta does well in rough weather, for the waves disguise the nylon leader and the rod outlined against the sky, and the bulk of the angler is distorted. The trout concentrates so fully on the fly dragging over the water surface, dipping and rising in the waves, that takes and boiling turns occur only a few feet from the fisherman. The fly does not do so well in rough water if fished in the point position on the cast; this is better occupied by a Black & Peacock Spider or a small Sweeney Todd. The point fly rarely breaks the surface film until the lift off into the back cast – thus the skidding effect of a dropper is lost.

The dropper drag does not work so well in the calm of an evening rise because the disturbance of the leader and dropper nylon is visible in the calm conditions. By all means, fish the Invicta at dusk in July and August but on the point as the only fly, and tweaked slowly in the retrieve. As to the size of hook, a No. 12 is generally a successful choice, although a No. 10 could be fished for sea trout from a boat in a Scottish loch. At night, in rivers, a better size for peal would be a No. 8.

The Invicta is not a hot weather fly in still waters. Sedges hatch at the water surface where they become airborne. Trout will not be found in the top water level in a heat wave; they will seek out the cooler depths which are not the places for hatching sedges. In consequence one must match the fly to the weather. The summer of 1982 was wet and windy; ideal conditions for the Invicta. During that season we caught 160 trout on the fly out of a recorded total of 320 exceeding 1 lb. The following year, 1983, was hot through the summer months. We still caught trout, over 300 of 1 lb and above, but many were taken deep down on large lures, mostly black in colour, on sinking fly lines. That season the Invicta managed no more than 35 victims, and these mostly at the end of September and into October when the rains came after the equinox.

The Red Sedge

26 September 1987. Fernworthy. 8 brown trout. Total 9 lb 6 oz. Best 1 lb 5 oz. A fine end to our brown trout season. George, Simon, Mandy and Phillip, 1 fish each. Myself 4. All on No. 12 dry Red Sedge and 5X knotless tapered leaders. The osprey, still present after one week, watched us with interest and made a fruitless dive.

The osprey, probably a bold but inexperienced bird of the year, must have been on migration from the nesting areas of Scotland to Africa. I have seen them before, these birds of passage, in the south on the Hampshire Avon. We did not notice this fish hawk take a trout but, unconcerned by anglers, he quartered the lake at a slow flap. A sinister bird – angular wings, all-seeing eyes, black and white – but the streamlined, arrowed final gathering-in of the wings for the dive into water is grace at its most purposeful. Up he came fishless, long wings lifting the body by wide sweeps from the water which he shook in a spray from his feathers whilst airborne.

We fished in the north bay with the wind blowing parallel to the shore. Dry flies cast out at right angles to the bank drifted around in an arc; and the trout took them. The Red Sedge is a great favourite with us. Winged or hackled, well-waterproofed, and fished off a fine leader, it is irresistible to surface feeding trout. A No. 12 is a good hooking size – more rises develop into rod-bending trout, but the playing must be delicate on a 5X point. For myself it is one fish per fly which is then discarded. There is no reward for fishing wet bedraggled specimens which have already done their duty. Trout like a Cinderella needle pointed foot upon the water film; a soggy fly must have a track like gum boots when viewed from below. Of course, we were fortunate, as our flies are tied in Kenya by Jim Chege, to whom I send the hooks. Back come the flies, seven or eight hundred at a time: pristine specimens, gossamer examples of a skilled dresser's work.

At one time on still waters I took a leaf from the river dry-fly man's book and fished a dragless imitation. No sedge of mine would create ripples on the water. Today, on lakes, I induce a little movement: this draws the trout as though to a struggling insect. A pull of one yard on the floating line momentarily sends out an attractive wave behind the fly. The trout, investigating, arrives when the fly is once more still, settled and the nylon no longer apparent through movement. One is always learning. The month before this day I watched a boy draw his Red Sedge across the surface almost to his feet – a following trout, which could not be seen approaching, took as the water shallowed out and the fly neared escape. Drag seems to have a place in the tactics of the still-water dry-fly man.

These trout were stocked brownies, and we kept our catch on the basis of 'what they have put in for us we might as well take out', there being little food for them in that water in the winter. Although we kept them, they were not well conditioned trout, for the end of the brown trout season was at hand and the hens were gravid. If they had been river fish they would have been returned to spawn, but in lakes, particularly with a bed of peat or soft mud, the environment into which they have been introduced is unsuitable for extensive breeding, and the acid water holds little food.

Four grilse

7 September 1987. Dart. 4 grilse. Total 19 lb 8 oz. 1-in. Copper Dart. No. 1 grilse top of Wide Pool to Bob at 11.30 am. No. 2 second stickle above to myself at noon. No. 3 in Rock Pool to Bob after lunch, although we had covered the lie before without result. All 3 netted. No. 4 in Saucepan Handle to myself at 1.45 pm, tailed by Brian who arrived on the scene (this fish risen 11.00 am had dropped back 5 yd downstream). All grilse on same Copper Dart, but new treble each time. Water dirty on arrival at 9.00 am after previous day's rain, but cleared by 11.00 am when fish first took interest. Ceased, satisfied, at 2.00 pm and went home. Bob's first two salmon on fly. We shared one rod, taking turns to fish and photograph the other. Next day hooked and lost a grilse on No. 4 silver upstream Mepps.

59 *Bob Sinclair-Taylor plays the first grilse of his life taken on fly.* (7 September 1987)

'Look,' I said to Bob on the telephone the previous evening, 'I'm short of September action salmon pictures for the book. Can't guarantee anything as there may not have been enough rain. Will you meet me in Tavistock at 8.00 am tomorrow? We'll take two cameras, one rod, a net, sandwiches and beer, and drive across the moor. Fly only today. Spinning tomorrow. Are you on?'

We parked Bob's Land Rover just outside the town and went on in my car, swapping fishing experiences and sorting out a plan of action. The Tavy and its tributary, the Walkham, were low when we crossed their bridges – it didn't look too promising. At the Dart my marker rock was just awash; if there had been a finger joint of depth, I would have been confident, for there are always fish about in September. All one requires to take them are rainfalls sufficient to raise the river by three or four inches. In addition to flow, water colour is a telling factor. There was too much colour in the Dart when we arrived, in fact the river ran a heavily-stained brown, but stain, unlike suspended matter, is no bad thing, because clarity increases rapidly on that river. Exceptional clarity is

60 *I hook the second grilse . . . (7 September 1987)*

61 *which leaps. . .*

62 *I lift it out by pressing in the gill flaps*

more often a problem than too much turbidity. The water will often clear within hours, and that proved to be the case as we worked our way upriver.

Bob wears leather boots when fishing in places where much walking is required, wrapping these with waterproof gaiters from ankle to knee. Those canvas gaiters by Berghouse are worth a second glance: they terminate at the lower end in a close-fitting rubber skin, which grips under the boot instep, encloses the tongue and eyeholes and clings with waterproof tenacity around the calves. One has all the comfort of leather footwear and the water tightness of a gum boot. Moving up the river we took turns with the rod at the lies on reaching each likely place; one casting whilst the other held the camera at the ready. At 11.30 am I positioned Bob on a mid-stream boulder, joining him myself as he cast a short line into the foam and turbulence at a pool run-in. Through polaroids, after several fruitless casts, I saw his first grilse rise and take, turn and go down. 'Raise your rod', I urged, cupping my hand under the bottom section to lift the tip. Bob was astonished, 'Crikey. I didn't see a thing, but he's on!' I left him to make his own way to the bank from where it would be easier to handle the fish, but placed the Gye net where he could reach it easily before taking up the cameras. This first salmon of Bob's life on fly was a triumph for which he had worked with diligence over two seasons.

The second fish came to me half an hour later. This grilse lifted from the river bed and turned beneath the fly without taking. In these circumstances the lure should be presented again, two or three times, perhaps with a sink and draw

63 Bob hooks his second grilse . . .

64 *As it thrashes, Bob should now enter the river to be on a level with the fish . . .*

65 *He reaches forward from the top of the bank . . .*

66 *The rod bends dangerously because he is way up above the fish . . .*

67 *He lifts the net, putting too much strain on the aluminium net shaft, which could break. The shaft should be held close to the net rim*

68 *All is accomplished and he cuts out the tube fly treble*

variation. This proved tempting, up he came in the dangle position, sank back and I raised the rod as his head went down. Bob then took several shots of the fighting fish.

An hour passed in which we fished and then ate lunch sitting on the bank – the water at our feet was clearing all the time. Covering three more pools without response we turned for home. On the way Bob tried the neck of a pool where we had no luck on the way up. This time a salmon was at home. No problems arose in the hooking of the second fish; Bob saw the rise, paused, tightened when the salmon straightened the line, and the hooks went home. Not so the netting. The photographs revealed with clarity the problems which arise in netting a salmon if the angler is much above the level of the fish – Bob was on a high bank. With rod bent like a bow, he eventually slid the salmon over the net rim and lifted the fish onto the bank. In so doing he might have snapped the rod and bent the aluminium net shaft. If he had been in the water at the same level as the salmon the rod would have drawn the fish to the net, rather than lifted it over the rim, and the salmon could then have been dragged to the side in the net bag without straining the shaft by a lifting action. However, he wasn't in waders. Clearly leather boots are best for walking and waders for fishing, but there is a compromise solution. In summer when the weather is really hot and long boots uncomfortable I buy a cheap pair of thigh boots and cut them off level with the bend of the knee. Such a semi-wader is 8

69 The fourth grilse. Brian arrives on the scene and tails the fish . . .

70 *Success at last!*

in. longer than a standard gum boot and sufficient for most netting situations.

By now we were both slightly euphoric: three grilse and a fine selection of shots in both black and white and colour. We would go home, trying a salmon risen in the morning on the way back. When a fish has come to the fly without a touch and then shows no more interest despite the wiles of the angler; different patterns of fly; altered speed of retrieve; sink and draw; and other methods such as mending in both directions, it may be that the fish is no longer in the original position. If this is so the salmon has usually dropped downstream by a few yards rather than moved upriver. That had been the action of the fourth fish which came up from a nook about six yards below the original lie. He was hooked and led upstream, but after a minute or two ran down towards a danger area. At this stage a quiet voice asked over my shoulder, 'Like me to tail him Charles?' Brian had appeared unnoticed and I was relieved to see him. Brian knows what he is doing! Here was a chance of photographs of a tailer in action, and with Brian there was little risk, even with the wire-noosed tailer on the slimness of a grilse. The fish was manoeuvred below his stand, the wire loop swiftly and discreetly encircled the tail and moved up the body above the adipose fin. A flick of the wrist, a sharp pull, an elbow raised, a flurry of spray and the grilse was on the bank.

After each salmon we replaced the Partridge X3 No. 8 outpoint treble, but retained the original tube fly. The X3 is a splendid hook with needle points and fine penetrating wire – that wire will bend out if subjected to undeserved stress. Perfect as the hooks looked after each landing I replaced them, for one of the trebles may have caught in a net mesh and been very slightly weakened. This action, or habit, may suggest over-caution, for I have the highest regard for Partridge and use their trebles in all my tube flies. It is a matter of relative values: a few pence for a hook or the slight chance of losing a salmon.

Two salmon to one angler is about the wise limit for the month of September on the Dart – there are future seasons to be considered. Whilst it makes no difference to salmon propagation whether a fish is removed from the river at the beginning or the end of the season, either being a loss to the spawning beds, the autumn fish may be soft fleshed and of second rate value on the table.

When we returned to the water marker rock by the car we found the river level unchanged. Our success was almost certainly owing to a run of new grilse and the stain of colour in the water.

Two salmon from the lower Itchen

The Itchen is not solely a dry-fly brown-trout chalk stream. Sea-liced salmon are caught in the lower reaches on fly, worm, prawn and spinning baits. This account of a September day was sent to me by Tony Allen, who fishes there regularly with Brian, a friend of his.

It was clearly going to be a fine day. The sun shone on arrival and their dogs, two yellow labradors and a red setter, greeted each other boisterously once out

Otter

of the cars, before hunting out the water voles which make holes in the river banks. Tony and Brian sat on benches at the rustic table to enjoy a dram as the river drifted by. The water was clear, and thus it would be easy to spot salmon on their lies, but there was a disappointing volume of dying weed coming down the river, and more was being pulled up by the resident swans. This weed would make fly fishing almost impossible. There is little more irritating than constantly clearing the fly of bits and pieces. Plainly, they would have to fish the prawn and an upstream Mepps or Toby.

On this particular day they made a plan: Brian would drive to the lower end of the beat, leave the car, and fish up to meet Tony who would work downstream. At the half-way point there would be a meeting for sharing experiences and information on the positions of reluctant salmon. Brian would then continue up, and Tony down the river. One could not help feeling sorry for the salmon at this point in the narrative for Tony is a master of the prawn, and Brian likes the flash of a two- or three-inch gold or silver Toby which he chucks upstream over the salmon's heads and then retrieves back fast.

To fish the prawn successfully requires preparation – sometimes weeks or months in advance using fresh small tough, long-legged, whiskered English specimens. These are not available all year – the summer is their time, and Poole harbour the port of call. The doleful prawns in the fishmonger's tray have had the life beaten out of them. They are overcooked, resultantly soft-bodied, and usually short of legs and whiskers. Often they are too large and, almost without exception, fall to pieces after a few casts on the prawn mount. In addition, one needs a small prawn in the summer when the river is warm. Buy 2 or 3 lb of fresh English prawns brought in by boat from the sea that morning. These will be enough for a season or two. Cook them yourself until they just turn pink but not soft, spread them out on a rough towel and dry them with a hair dryer. Packaged in half dozens and frozen they will keep for many months. Take them to the river in an ice-packed vacuum flask, still in their polythene packs and then, if unused, they may be returned to the freezer at the day's end.

Tony mounted his prawn with a single Partridge No. 6 outpoint treble in the whiskers, a thin wire pin down the centre of the body, the nylon trace led between the separated legs, and the whole wrapped about from head to tail with fine copper wire unravelled from an electric cable. He broke off the spear of the prawn, in case this discouraged the salmon from taking hold at the hook end or the spear protected the hook, and removed the tail to prevent the prawn revolving in the current. This carefully prepared bait was then fished between the weed beds on a paternoster outfit with a ½-oz weight. Clearly, there is more to prawning than might be imagined. Skill is needed and yet the odds are on the fish, for on this day two salmon escaped after taking the bait and only the third customer was landed.

He approached the first pool on a long rickety platform, cast out the prawn into the current, which swung the outfit around whilst the weight tap-tapped on the bed of the river as the rod tip lifted and dropped at regular intervals. Half way down the pool, as the prawn was raised to the surface a salmon of 8 or 9 lb followed it up to the top, took, and then backed away. A cunning fish this one, which savoured the prawn and did not turn away to give Tony a chance to strike the hooks in from behind; instead he sank slowly from sight, mouth partly open, prawn visible. Something had to be done. Tony struck. The salmon came to the surface, head still up, mouth open, shook the prawn out of its jaws and was gone like a thief fading into the night. Should Tony have struck? Should he have given slack line instead in the hope that the salmon would turn to allow a more effective hook setting, and if he had done so would the salmon have ejected the bait in those out of contact seconds? There can be no sure answer. Prawn fishing is neither simple nor constantly productive.

Then there was the second fish, which could be seen close in to the bank in three or four feet of water. A pale fresh salmon a rod's length from the bankside rushes. With care he could be reached. Stealing forward, on his knees, Tony lowered the prawn to within a foot of the salmon's nose. The fish, blandly and with a smug expression at so foolhardy an action on the part of a spearless defenceless prawn, opened its jaws to allow the prawn to drift inside the white lipped mouth. The rod arched up, the fish turned down river, ran away and . . . was off! Not a good start to the day, but typical of prawn fishing.

When the two anglers met half way down the beat, Brian reported that five salmon had chased his Toby, but none had plucked up a final thrust of courage to take the lure. Walking together back to the top of the beat the day was so bright and sunny that everything could be seen in detail in the clear water. With their experience they had not expected the bankside salmon to return to her lie after the momentary hooking which had taken place half an hour before, but there she was! Again she took and this time the treble went home, the salmon fled, leaped, splashed and stood on her tail, but to no avail because soon she was in Brian's net. Weighed at lunch she pulled the spring balance down to 7½ lb. As Tony said, it is not often a fish will take twice in so short a space of time – perhaps, originally, she never felt the hooks at all or maybe the prawn had just been gripped across the body. This happens, I have seen the action myself with a prawn and also a long tube fly. A salmon's jaws can tweak and grip with accuracy.

Tony and Brian then broke off for lunch, setting out a picnic on the table under the trees. By now it was like a mid-summer day but with the crispness of autumn, tranquillity enveloped them, and satisfaction stole over them at the sight of the salmon on the grass. After lunch they fished in turn down the same bank, but Brian exchanged the Toby for a paternoster outfit with large lob worms on a No. 2 Mustad beak hook – there is no doubt that salmon become educated when regularly presented with worms and prawns. Some may have been pricked and escaped. Others have been frightened by incautious clumsy anglers. This may have been the case with a fish they saw of 15 or 16 lb lying under a streamer of weed. They waited for the current to waft the streamer to one side, then presented the prawn – but the fish would have none of it and disappeared for good.

At times and in deep places they fished the water, searching for salmon, sweeping the pools, hoping for a tweak or pull. From one deep hole behind a groyne the worm induced a solid take. There was no doubt about this one: the rod did not spring straight; the hook did not fly back; the net was wetted; and the fish was on the bank. They were almost a pair, those salmon. The second just touched the 7-lb mark, and, although neither had sea lice, their silver sheen indicated a recent upriver departure from Southampton Water to the Itchen.

The day was called to an end when a chill mist rolled up the river. As the dogs, twitching and dreaming, slept in the cars, two anglers, tired but complete, went home with a salmon apiece. The Itchen, lonely in the failing light, flowed on towards the sea.

The last of the season's peal

3 September 1982. Dart. Julian had 3 peal by the pipe in Carradon Ford. Two on 1-in. Alexandra tubes and one on a 1-in. Silver Stoat's Tail. 1 lb 8 oz, 1 lb 2 oz and 12 oz

and:

12 September 1982. Dart. I had 1 peal opposite the pipe in Carradon Ford and 1 in the tail of Carradon Turn. 1 lb 3 oz and 1 lb 1 oz. 1-in. Silver Stoat's Tail tube.

Our beat on the lower Dart is a day or two's swim for a sea trout from the tidal waters of the estuary, or half an hour by air from the sea as the cormorant flies. Peal are therefore fresh, bright and generally firm fleshed, even in September. They taste good, too, with the tang of the sea in their meat. These desirable table qualities are not present if they are caught in the latter half of September on the high moor, or far up one of the lowland rivers like the Tamar. Such fish may be dark skinned and have soft, pale flesh. Even on our beat I am not keen on taking sea trout later than the middle of the month and, in any case, the rough weather of the equinox on 22/23 September effectively calls a halt to pleasant fishing in the night. The first 10 days, or 12 at the most, are our last chance. If there is a full moon not only does this keep one company in the long dark hours but the high spring tide brings in an extra run of sea trout. On 5 and 7 September 1979 three of us had fourteen peal to 3 lb 6 oz and four brown trout with a total weight of 19 lb 14 oz. All these were caught on 1-in. Alexandra tubes and Silver Stoat's Tails. On those two nights the moon was so bright that we could see every fish which moved, pinpoint the position and cast to individual peal with accuracy.

Back to Julian on 3 September. At that time he must have been in his early 'teens, very dedicated to fly fishing and a grand caster. Julian could throw out a long line when it pleased him, and was necessary, using a 9 ft 3-in. fibreglass reservoir rod with a butt extension which he tucked up his sleeve to strengthen his wrist. His system at night was to tie on a 1-in. Alexandra tube at the point of a home-made leader tapered to 9 lb. With this outfit, and a net at his waist, he would wade out 3 or 4 yd into the river to stand on a spit of sand. He then cast diagonally across upstream into the deep water under the far bank. There is a lie there, much favoured by peal large and small, which Julian knew about. He then retrieved faster than the current, intent for a take, eyes searching, fingers sensitive. He rarely came back empty handed from that place. On one occasion he fished from dusk to dawn, a rare dedication, taking three fish to 2 lb 12 oz. He told me later that 'things hotted up' half an hour before the return of daylight.

So, sea trout fishing in September can be rewarding. In 1986 the total peal catch from the 18 rivers of the South West Water region for the month was only beaten by the catch in July and August. In 1985 the take by rods for the month was 731 peal, almost equal to June at 735, out of a regional total of 4535 for the four months of June to 30 September. The sea trout season ends on 30 September for almost all the South West rivers – the only notable exception being the Teign which closes on 12 October. It is years since I fished the Teign, and that is an omission I ought to rectify, for the peal catches are higher than in any other river in the area, although the Fowey, in Cornwall, runs a good second, followed by the Camel and the Taw.

Well, all good things come to an end. Now is the time to say goodbye to the peal until we meet, by chance, a large member of that elusive tribe when salmon spinning in the second half of March, or later on in April. On such thoughts we muse and dream whilst tying our tube flies through the winter, creating plain honest lures: slim singles, and tubes straggly with peacock herl, but shining with hope and silver tinsel.

Salmon on the fly in a gale

28 September 1982. Dart. With Adrian and Helen.
10.30 am. Top of Iron Bars. 7¹/₂ lb. 1-in. Copper Dart.
2.00 pm. Sycamore Hole. 7 lb. 1¹/₄-in. Black Dart.
3.30 pm. Wide Pool, in middle. 8¹/₂ lb. 1¹/₄-in. Black Dart.

That was a wet and windy day if ever there was one. We were soaking by tea-time, and I had lost my deerstalker hat, when it was blown clean off my head into the river. We tried to hook it out by casting tube flies at the crown whilst it floated, but the wind prevented all attempts. The rain, therefore, ran down my neck, but this didn't matter; our blood was up, we had three salmon on the bank. I can't remember much about the first two catches, but the river was probably rising because I increased the fly size for the second and third salmon. The third fish and the two losses which preceded it are clear memories.

There is nothing quite so helpful in a wide pool as a strong upstream gale lashing the water into rolling waves. Provided you can throw out a long line, it matters little if splash is created as the line bashes down on the water, or for that matter if you stand silhouetted against the sky – the waves conceal all. Your

71 *Three salmon of 7¹/₂ lb, 7 lb and 8¹/₂ lb taken on Black Dart tubes in a gale. Dart*
(28 September 1982)

task is to propel your fly over the water towards the far bank and then strip it back at speed. The fly will be invisible to you most of the time in the breaking waves and the line/leader junction knot will be lost in spume, but you will see the black back of a rolling salmon. That you cannot miss. Whether he has taken the fly or missed it in the flurry, only time will tell – those two seconds after he goes down when the line does, or does not, straighten with a jerk. And it will be a jerk with the fish travelling at speed. There is no finesse in the hooking; all is in the lap of the gods. One waits two seconds and one sees. The first two fish at 3.30 pm in Wide Pool were hooked momentarily and must have returned discomforted and at speed to the lie. Sometimes a frightened fish will disturb others but not in a gale. No messages of fear were passed. They just lined up. One after the other. If I cannot have a wet day for salmon, give me a windy one.

The following day was fine and bright, but there was still colour in the water as Adrian fished the first stickle above Concrete Post. He took a salmon of 10½ lb, his first, on a 1-in. Copper Dart. We had fished over the stickle an hour earlier, but in the meantime the sun had come off the water, dropping behind the hill. It is clear that the river was falling away from the level of the previous day for a small tube, the 1-in. Copper Dart, was the successful lure.

Final salmon of the Dart season

30 September 1984. Dart. Heavy spate at 8.15 am. Fished down to Stoney on left bank. Not a fin. Whilst having lunch by myself, saw a fish move in tail of pool under right bank below central rock. Crossed river higher up. Took cock fish in tail of the sandy run-off at 1.00 pm. 1½-in. Black Dart. 5½ lb.

One has to be lucky to take a cock fish on the final day. If a hen had come my way I would have put her back, for one likes to end the season with a glow of righteousness.

The capture came about in this manner. The river was really too full, and all the fish were travelling. Some of them rolled in unusual places, one or two showed a dorsal fin for a second or two, but this little cock was different. He showed his tail – for no more than two seconds. The distance from me was considerable, certainly 100 yards, but one develops an awareness, a knowledge of where to direct your eye, and an out of place movement in the water, be it ever so small, is at once apparent. This tail showed as he lifted over a ridge of rock and slid down into two or three feet of water, a shallow place, not a place to stay for long because the water would fall away. But, I judged, you will stay there for half an hour, and that is all I need to walk half a mile upstream, ford the river with a piece of driftwood as a prop, come down and catch you. He did not let me down: he swirled in a copper gleam as the large tube swung across his window and the rod in my hands bent into a curve and bucked against my belt. Always helpful, he allowed me to walk him up

72 *Lara's first salmon on a fly. 10 lb. 1¼-in Black Dart tube fly* (29 September 1984)

73 *The final fish of the season. 5½-lb grilse.* (30 September 1984)

away from danger, over yellow sandbanks covered with shallow peaty water carrying twirling autumn leaves, to the deepness of the netting place. I pocketed him and walked home to tea. It is not often one takes a salmon on a river's final day.

A case for barbless fish hooks

30 September 1980. West Dart. Bill, George and myself caught 3 small brownies on dry fly.

This was the first day of fly fishing for both Bill and George. They were not disconcerted by the small size of the West Dart browns. 'It doesn't matter. It's a trout. Any trout will do', they said. Why I set them to fish dry fly upstream, the most difficult method, as an introduction is beyond memory. Perhaps they looked abnormally capable! They were certainly exhilarating company, and were probably taken because this was the last day of the river brown trout season and they would not have otherwise had the experience. It was enjoyable, fishing upstream dry fly in the isolation of a moorland stream with whirling holes, lichen-encrusted boulders, the bright red berries on the mountain ash, and the chunky dipper bobbing on a rock at water level. Of course, there is also a sadness as we shall not be fishing there again until April at the earliest, it is too cold in March, and today the season ends for salmon, peal, and the darting red-spotted native wild brown trout.

As I remember the day we started by fishing the downstream wet fly: Greenwell's Glory, Peter Ross, Black & Peacock Spider. Any of these will induce the trout to pluck at the fly, to dimple at the surface, perhaps to hook themselves as the little lure twists, lifts, swings and moves with the current. We return the trout which are usually too small to eat, unless the cat fancies one, in which case it is cleaned in the river and taken home in a polythene bag in my poacher's pocket.

Hook and release, a practice made readily possible by barbless hooks, was not widely promoted in the early 1980s. The system could be adopted with advantage on the West Dart, so far as the small brown trout are concerned. It is so easy to damage these little fish, some of which may prove on examination to be salmon parr. Barbless or not, at least the unhooking should be carried out underwater and without contact with the rough meshes of a landing net. Flies with barbless hooks are not widely available in the tackle shops, but there is nothing to stop us pressing in the barb with a pair of snipe-nosed pliers before we start.

The diary records that the three brown trout were taken on dry fly, but we started downstream wet. This is because a higher percentage of trout are hooked if taken from behind by casting upstream dry or, for that matter, upstream wet. Furthermore one is less visible fishing at a lower level than the trout. All the arguments, the telling factors, must be in favour of the upstream dry fly unless the water is cold, when depth is the only answer. There is not a lot to be said for fishing on the high moor for trout in cold weather – the practice is unrewarding and the fingers grow white with cold on the cork butt of the rod. The season is ending and we must leave the river to the mergansers which fly up and down the valley, the stalking heron, the diminutive teal which spring in fast lifting haste from a ditch or flash of water, and the mallard which are mouth-waterly plump. The weed beds will die away, mud will be scoured by the winter floods and the crisp brown leaves of wind blackened beech trees will be swirled away by wind and water in October. Sheep will remain to crop the coarse grass of the river bank, and ponies, the wild ones of the moor, will gallop free in the thickness of winter coats. We shall be back in six or eight weeks' time to walk the river, to watch in wonder as salmon and peal renew the cycle of life on the gravel spawning beds.

CHAPTER 8

OCTOBER

In this month fishing locations must be chosen with care and the fish species selected with discrimination, for the breeding weeks are not long hence. The brown trout season in rivers generally ends on 30 September in England and Wales, although some water authority regions continue into October, and in Scotland the final fishing day is on the 6th. The angler is advised to enquire, for not only are the regulations different in some areas, but there may be a distinction between brown trout (also described as non-migratory) in rivers and still waters. In my home county of Devon the river season for non-migratory trout closes on 30 September, whilst in enclosed waters –that is, lakes and reservoirs– the end does not come until the 12th of the month. Personally, I have no

Mepps spoon

wish to take brown trout in October. They have provided us with fascinating fishing for six and a half months, and now is the time to respect their privacy as they lose condition, becoming swollen with eggs or milt. An October brown trout is seldom worth eating and, in still waters, there may not be much skill in locating and hooking the males which wait, aggressively, at the entrances to those spawning streams which run into the lake.

Also, ask when the season closes for rainbow trout. Normally there is no close season in enclosed waters, and in some rivers you may fish for them throughout the year. In a few rivers, those where rainbows breed, there may be a close season. This is the case in the Trent area of the Severn-Trent Water Authority in respect, amongst others, of the Derbyshire Wye. In the area of the Welsh Water Authority there is no close season in still waters, but in rivers the fishing ends on 30 September and does not re-open until the 3 March.

Leaving aside the regulations, what will be the quality and the ethics of taking rainbow trout in October, and then on throughout the winter? This all depends upon the trout with which the water has been stocked: some fish will be losing condition. A red-flanked cock rainbow with a long lower jaw, terminating in a savage kype, is not a desirable occupant of any dinner plate! Triploids are different. These are sexless rainbows which retain condition, being always bright, sparkling and good to eat. My personal inclination is to take rainbows throughout the month if they are in fair condition, and then close my season until the following March.

There is still good salmon fishing in a minority of rivers – those with a genuine autumn or winter run coming in from the sea. Rivers in this category in the south west of England include the Fowey, Camel and Plym. Additionally, there are those whose seasons just finish in October, such as the Tamar, the Tavy, and the rivers of Wales. In Scotland the variations are between 30 September and the end of November. It is a good idea to buy the Thomas Harmsworth directory **Where to Fish**; this gives detailed information, but even then enquiries should be made, for closing dates vary and there are many rivers.

On some late rivers in both the north and south of the British Isles not only is there a genuine autumn run, but most salmon will then be taken for the whole season – and this includes entries of heavy, late running grilse. To fish where allowed in the autumn months is accepted practice, but I urge you to take no more than you need. I have written that it makes no difference to the numbers on the spawning beds whether a fish is taken at the beginning or the end of the season, but there is a difference in the fish. Some are not worth eating. Take one or two, preferably cock fish, and have them smoked. Do not become one of those anglers who is photographed proudly by a row of ten swollen-bellied fish – for so many to be caught means the fishing is easy. Remember the anti-sporting groups, and our own urgings of moderation which we press upon the netsmen.

*

October is welcomed by many as the month in which, following the closure of trouting on the premier chalkstreams, anglers may be allowed on these waters to fish by fly or bait for grayling. This will be inexpensive or even free, requiring a high degree of skill and, thus, challenge. October has much to offer: golden days, falling leaves, frosts and a log fire in the evening.

A grayling day

6 October 1987. River Test. Bossington. 1 rainbow of 2 lb 13 oz and 4 grayling. We returned a number of brown trout after removing the fly with artery forceps. The grayling had the same treatment. Just kept the one large rainbow which had a fine tail.

74 *Tony Allen playing a grayling on a 8-ft split cane fly rod. River Test.* (6 October 1987)

75 *Tony trotting for grayling. River Test* (6 October 1986)

76 *Head keeper Brian Parker (standing in boat) removes a fallen tree from the river. River Test* (6 October 1986)

I have never seen so many fish in a river: brown trout, rainbows, grayling and a leaping salmon. And why not? As Brian Parker, the head riverkeeper, says, 'There's plenty of natural food for all.' He likes to see a few grayling, and so do I, for this summer spawning fish comes into winter fighting trim when the trout are intent on marital matters. And grayling are wonderful sporting fish if taken on fine tackle, and very tasty, too, if you remove the scales.

Five of us met at 10.30 am on that day at the Beat No. 6 fishing hut, with more water to cover down the river than we could possibly manage. The river was alive with rises to pale wateries, blue-winged olives and a few skittering sedges as one or the other hatched throughout the day. We tied a No. 14 Wickham's Fancy to a 5X leader for Bill, who, being the senior one amongst us, started first. We then followed with like outfits after something taken to warm the inner man and celebrate the day.

Tony was into a grayling almost at once below the bridge. He was likely to set us an example, not only because he works on and knows the river, but owing to fine nylon – a gossamer thread. Trout and grayling just cannot see his leader, or so one imagines from the number which he fools, but then, you see, the breaking strain of the tippet is only 1.9 lb. It is amazing how much strain such a point will take if you hook your fly into a stump and pull – few grayling or trout could beat such drag.

For myself, I opted for a riverside downstream walk, watching all the time, keeping back from the bank, taking the river's pulse. I made a start by casting up along the edge of a line of piling. There were trout there, rising, and grayling too. It is possible to distinguish the rises of one fish from the other. The grayling spends his time on the river bed, rising steeply to take a fly. His disturbance of the surface is a little sharper than the roll of a trout. Oh those trout! Their backs were broad, their tails wide, and the big bubbles they left behind were tremendous. But the fish rising in line ahead by the piling would have nothing to do with me. They didn't want to know – they were educated. A rash fish would have to be found, a less selective mid-river monster better suited to my 13-stone methods. I walked and looked and studied. Then he rose above a bar of weed – nose, dorsal fin and then the tail. One section at a time. He may not have been a true alderman amongst his brothers in the Test but to me, used to the 6-in. West Country boys, he appeared majestic in the size and slowness of the royal taking roll. My fly landed, as I thought, just right and right it was – but not for him. Some whippersnapper, a brash minion, the fly-half behind a solid member of the rugger pack, snitched my Wickham and dived into the weeds. The usurper was released after causing disruption in the royal swim. He had at least proved the fly was right. I fished on down to give the king time to recover his poise. A covey of partridge crossed the Test, landed, and made creaking calls as they ran across the field on the other side. A water vole caused excitement with his waves and sploshing under the bank: surely, here was a fish of substance which would match the disappointment of the king – but ratty disappeared.

I retraced my steps to the royal swim and, to my relief, he was there, feeding.

If the fly-half hadn't upset him neither would my casting. On went a new fly with pristine hackles, the best to be found in the Wickham compartment of the Wheatley fly box. After dipping this in the floatant bottle, I gave a few sharp puffs to blow the hackles dry and launched the fly. It landed with delicacy in just the right place, one yard above the royal nose. The king looked, lifted, took – and set off for the sea. He wouldn't be stopped. We went down river, sometimes running, at others ambling, but down we went. He had a liking for weedbeds: I pulled him out. He preferred the other bank: I coaxed him back to mine. A drifting lump of weed settled on the leader where it troubled him less than me. When he quietened down close by I crept forward on my knees and pulled the weed off the nylon – otherwise the rod could not be raised to draw him close for the final act, the netting. And he was netted and taken back to the fishing hut with a piece of red baler twine through his gills.

What a lunch awaited us at the hut: chickens, salads with dressings, hot baked and buttered potatoes in tin foil, cheeses, wines and coffee. Our efforts at the grayling after lunch were enjoyable but incapable – we should have fished with a float and trotted down a maggot on a tiny single hook. One may sit to do this and dream a little as the red cork bobs upon the water. We fished in this manner the previous year on an early October day using a 12-ft rod, fixed spool reel, a shot or two to sink the bait and a nylon point of 1-lb breaking strain. This is fascinating fishing just below a weir in turbulent water. The rod swings out the float and the bait sinks to the grayling facing upstream like short grey arrows on the light chalk river bed. If you cannot see them you can imagine them in a shoal. And then the float slides away over the surface, submerges, and you life the rod with the delicate tip to play him tenderly, terrified all the time by the fineness of the nylon.

After tea the day grows cold, a chill breeze blows up the valley and the river stills. Cock pheasants call and clatter to roost; lights glow from cottage windows. We say goodbye and thank you to Brian for our day on the river which he tends throughout the year.

An October salmon from the River Lyd

10 October 1984. Oak Tree Pool. 2.30 pm. Lara hooked and played by herself. No. 2 Mepps. 8 lb.

The River Lyd is narrow where it runs below my house and then disappears down the valley to join the Tamar at Lifton; the water widens all the way. Our valley is an area of beauty, outstanding beauty: oak trees, beech trees, firs and farmhouses, fords, mills and fields. Wildlife is present in great variety – certainly greater than on Dartmoor where there is little for wild creatures to eat in winter. We have red deer with outstanding heads, and the smaller roe which strip the saplings of their bark. October is the time when the red stags roar – a

77 *8-lb salmon, taken on No. 2 Mepps. River Lyd (10 October 1986)*

78 *Cleaning an October salmon from the Lyd*

coughing grunt as they gather up their hinds and challenge their rivals. As the light fades in the evening and the dogs are taken for their final walk you may turn an ear to the stags in the woods which line the valley and run down to the river. There are badgers too, digging their setts into the hillsides and piling up the earth outside the holes. I have two of their skulls on a windowsill in my rod room which I retrieved from the river, they were washed clean by the water and scoured out by the drifting grit.

Then there are the winter birds. The dashing sparrowhawk is lethal as he glides down a narrow lane three feet above the road before lifting over the hedge to clutch in iron talons a defenceless finch or blackbird. Buzzards mew in the sky, their plaintive call echoing down the valley almost before first light. No doubt they like to be airborne in time for daybreak when they fall out of the sky upon an unwary rabbit, returning to a burrow in the hedge without an upward glance. The kingfishers never leave us and neither do the dippers which course along the twisting river, but other birds arrive in the soft muddied valley – those with long probing beaks. When frosts harden the east of England the woodcock and the snipe are our winter visitors. The woodcock's time is not yet; he will reach us with the first full November moon, and snipe come to the ditches of the west when the eastern fields freeze. Cattle start to be withdrawn from the grassland with the arrival of the autumn rains, to be replaced by sheep brought down from the bitter windswept moors where there is little grass. The feet of sheep are kinder to the soft land of the farmer's winter fields.

And so the scene changes, and now is our last chance to catch a salmon if we feel that way inclined. One will do, or two at the most, which we will smoke or make into pâté. One salmon is now my October ration from the Lyd, and then my role changes from predator to watcher in November and December when the salmon spawn.

It is always more pleasant and rewarding to take someone else fishing and for them to catch the fish. In September my daughter, Lara, caught her first salmon of 10 lb in the Dart on a 1¼ in. Black Dart – excitement enough, for her first salmon to be taken on a fly. But no, there was more to come. When the rains swept down our valley from grey slanting clouds on 8 October, pools of water formed in the low lying fields and the river roared under the old stone bridge below the house. Clearly there would be a run of salmon, and Lara had the chance to make it a double, in two days' time, by taking her second salmon on a spoon. The Lyd is small below our house and the banks are lined with trees. To fish the fly for salmon is barely possible, for there is hardly room to cast, other than with a short trout rod, and even then the fly tends to catch up in the trees. But the spoon, a small Mepps, is different. A Mepps may be flicked out with a ¼-oz weight and allowed to swing and flutter out of sight below the surface in the rushing narrow runs.

On the 10th we set off from the house together in waders, she with an 8 ft 6-in. fibreglass spinning rod, fixed spool reel, 18-lb monofilament line, a trace of 15-lb Platil and a No. 2 Mepps. That Mepps would have been the long model in copper, for this glints and matches the peaty tint of the river which rises on

Water vole

the north western slopes of Dartmoor. We started at the bathing pool where children swing on a car tyre, suspended from an overhanging tree in summer, and then fall laughing into the water to disturb my trout. The bathing pool was wide, smooth gliding and unresponsive. Yellow sycamore leaves swept down by the water gathered on the wires of a fence which the flood had submerged; others drifted on, appearing and disappearing as they lifted and then sank. Sometimes these leaves made our hearts pound if they twirled by our spinner, as we thought for a moment that they might be fish.

On we went, past the stump covered by the dog rose which bloomed delicate tinted pink flowers and in which a wren nested in May. We came to Oak Tree Pool which is where I hoped to take a salmon, but although Lara span this deep hole with care and the Mepps rose, fell, fluttered and enticed, there was no pull. We fished on to the end of the beat to the place where the water shallows below the manor house. A trout, a large one of 12 or 14 oz, gave us a moment of hope, but we shook him off the hook and fished back up the way we came. A sea trout jumped below a bush on an S-bend above a gravel bank; they too are in the river and intent on running up the valley. Like the brownies their season is past – they have earned their safety.

On our return to Oak Tree the water seemed a little clearer –the Lyd is a pure river, carrying little of the old red sandstone which makes many Devon rivers unfishable for three or four days after heavy rain. Out went the copper spoon. Lara concentrated on each flicked-out cast, lowering the rod tip when the bait had hit the water, winding slowly, swinging the rod from side to side to put a curve in the retrieve. Finally, she said 'I've got one Dad.' And she had.

Up came the rod tip whilst she wound the handle of the reel and the clutch slipped and clicked. 'It's no good winding all the time. You're putting twists in the line if the clutch slips' I said, and told her to pump up the rod tip and then wind as she momentarily dropped the rod point down a foot or two towards the water. The salmon was there in the deep of the pool, unknown in size, mysterious. Then he lifted, twisted and showed a silver side before the current swept him down from sight. Again the silver flashed –some fish, particularly grilse, run up very rapidly from the sea. The salmon swirled under our bank in a whirling backwater where the current ran upstream. She lifted him, pumped the rod, finger braking on the Mitchell spool. The fish came over the net rim, which I had extended in the backwater, and was drawn ashore. It was almost too much for Lara. Who has not known a sadness, a triumph, a regret and a pity – the blend is known to us all.

October rainbows and the Gold Muddler

6 October 1983. Fernworthy. With Bill and Bryan. 17 rainbows. 24 lb. All on Sweeney Todd with Gold Muddler on the bob. Best day this year.

Under the heading *The Invicta* in the September chapter, I discussed a method of fishing that fly as a dropper and the visual attraction of its colours. The fly is both an immitator and an attractor, and it is best to choose the size that matches a No. 12 hook. The point position on the cast being 'occupied by a Black & Peacock Spider or a *small* Sweeney Todd' in the team suggested for September.

In October the weather may not be rougher but the water will be colder, and this calls for a larger fly. Sedges are still hatching in small numbers, but the heyday of the sedge is over and we are entering weeks which are likely to be dominated by lure fishing on still waters, except when the sun is out and a warm breeze encourages a hatch of fly. October is a time when a particular lure, the Gold Muddler, will bring success. Fished off a floating line it will take over the position occupied by the smaller Invicta in September. The body of the fly is of flat gold tinsel and the head is made from a bunch of the body hair of a red deer. Deer's hair from the body of the animal has good floating qualities, which may be enhanced by the application of a floatant. We have, therefore, a lure which attracts in two ways: by the glint of the gold tinsel and by the small wake produced by the ruff or collar of the deer's hair head. This wake is at its most effective when the lure is fished in the bob, or top dropper, position and tripped over the water surface before the lift-off into the back cast.

It is interesting to note that on that day Bill took all this trout on the Sweeney Todd whilst most of mine came on the Gold Muddler. This can be explained by the length of our rods and the way in which we fished. Bill uses a 8 ft 6-in. split cane and fishes in gum boots; I use a longer rod and wade out in thigh boots. Equipped in this manner Bill does not, in fact cannot, effectively fish his Gold Muddler over the surface waves; his rod is too short for a final lure scuttle and he is too far from the deep water which trout are loath to leave. I had the advantage in both my off-shore position in my waders and my rod length so that I could attract trout in the final stages of each cast. We caught those trout on the north shore, in the angle between the bank and the dam. This is a place well suited to the bob fly because the bank inclines down steeply into deep water.

79 *Seventeen rainbows to Bill, Bryan and the author at Fernworthy. Sweeney Todd and Gold Muddler lures* (6 October 1983)

80 *Bill and Bryan prepare to take out a boat* (Fernworthy)

Trout following a dragged bob fly will come close to the north shore without the uneasiness they feel when following into shallow water. It is little use fishing the bob fly over a gently sloping bank, for the shallowness will deter trout from coming close enough for the angler to start the bob drag.

October rainbows and the Pheasant Tail Nymph

28 October 1983. Newhouse Fishery. Conall had his first trout on a Pheasant Tail Nymph he tied himself. Mrs Platts and myself 4 more. Total 5 fish of 9 lb 6 oz. The next day we had 2 more in the afternoon. 1 lb 8 oz and 1 lb 10 oz.

Newhouse is a small lake of four acres in a valley well protected by trees. Even at the end of October rainbows will rise consistently in the afternoon on mild days as the surface water warms a degree or two. If you arrive at ten or eleven o'clock in the morning you could be forgiven for thinking that the lake did not hold trout. After lunch you might have to eat your words. Such days occurred on 28 and 29 October 1983.

After lunch a trout bulged by the dam, then another where the old stream runs between the island and the bank, then they surfaced steadily, all over the place. There did not seem to be any floating flies as the fish were not leaving bubbles after a rise. A bubble is a sure sign of a fish taking floating flies – a mouthful of air is enclosed when the fly is engulfed, and then passes out through the gills as the trout goes down. There were no bubbles. Instead there were rolling backs and dorsal fins stretching the water skin: the trout were taking nymphs. On went No. 12 pheasant tail nymphs tied to the points of 8.5 lb Platil Strong home-made tapered leaders. We just put the nymph on the point, without adding a dropper or a bob.

We cast out onto the calm surface, the copper-bodied nymph cut through and sank below the water skin and back we tweaked the line – an inch or two at a time. The secret of this fishing lies in greasing the yard of leader closest to the fly line; the nylon then stays on the surface for the first yard but the rest is invisible. If you keep a sharp eye on this floating section you will note at once a twitch in the opposite direction to the retrieval – a trout has the nymph in his mouth! It is a satisfactory sight that forward pluck –only more pleasing is the flick of the wrist which sets the hook and causes the water to boil 15 yards away as the line lifts and tightens.

Rainbow trout on cold days

11 October 1981. Fernworthy. A jolly party with two boats. Bill and Bryan in one, Mike and myself in the other. Very rough and cold. Mike and I had 7 trout, 6 of them in half an hour in the afternoon in south east corner of the dam in a north west wind. Sinking lines. Total 8 rainbows, 1 brook trout. 9 lb 8 oz. Best 1 lb 8 oz. Most fish on No. 8 Black Chenille.

Here is further confirmation of the success of fishing in the area to which the wind is blowing. The north west wind was pushing warm water into the south east corner. We could not fish that corner in the morning because the boat's anchor dragged in the high wind, but in the afternoon there was a lull for an hour and we managed to hold the boat and cast our flies close to the dam and the shore in that corner. Rainbows had drifted there in considerable numbers, and we hauled them out. I doubt whether they would have taken in the morning if we had been able to reach that spot. In April and October the afternoon is best.

Rainbow trout on warm days

6 October 1978. Stafford Moor. Jim, Sue and Michael who had his first trout on dry fly. Total bag 5 rainbows, 11 lb 11 oz. Best 2 lb 10 oz. All on No. 14 Coch-y-Bondhu.

We fished that day in the corner of a 14-acre lake behind the belt of fir trees, choosing that area because a warm breeze was blowing towards us. I prefer to fish in a corner if the wind is filling it up with warm water, insects and, hopefully, trout. There was no logic to our choice of the Coch-y-Bondhu dry fly, which is an imitation of a Welsh beetle found in June, but these late rainbows don't know that the beetle is a member of the order Coleoptera, or that the mayfly is an Ephemeroptera. They are only used to the trout pellet and have much to learn of the devious and deceptive ways of fishermen – if they are given time to learn.

Michael took his first trout on this small black-hackled beetle which has a twist of gold tinsel at the tail, and we both agreed that he would not forget the experience. I can see that little black fly now, sitting innocently on the water, waiting for attention. It was not possible to see the 4X leader, attached to the waiting Michael. Then a black nose pushed up the water film, took down the fly and Michael, after a nerve racking pause, hooked it.

A measure of the thrill of deceiving a good trout with the dry fly is the manner in which the event occurs. Two days before we had taken five rainbows and one brown to a total of 12 lb 12 oz on sunk lures – and I can't recall one of those trout.

Salmon from the Deveron

If you would like a final fling at salmon before the winter, then try the River Deveron (north east Scotland). It is a fine long river which flows below the walls of Huntly castle, passes by Turriff and enters the sea between the towns of Banff and Macduff. My own fishing on the river has been on privately owned beats, but I have always wanted to stay in Huntly to fish the Burgh waters. Daily tickets are available from Monday to Friday from Murdoch, McMath and Mitchel, whose offices are in Juke Street. The licence must be purchased on the morning of the day on which you wish to fish, and private beats in the area may be reserved through Manson's tackle shop in Gordon Street.

The water at Huntly is attractive and clears more rapidly after heavy rain than the lower river close to the sea. For the whole river the rods take 75 per cent of the season's salmon catch in September and October, and in that latter month at Huntly fishing is limited to the spinner and the fly.

In 1980 I arranged a visit with three pupils to fish two lower beats whilst we stayed at The County Hotel in Banff. The hotel itself is very much a part of the pleasure of the holiday, for not only is it a fine Georgian house, but the food is excellent.

During our visit the river ran high for almost the whole of the first week, in the second half of which it was practically unfishable. In the first three days fortune smiled on us and we took three salmon. This group then left for the south, and I was joined by Bill and Tewdwr for the final three days of the season. Here is the record of our experiences:

20 October 1980. River Deveron. Scatterty beat, just above King Edward's Burn. Louise had her first salmon. 4 lb. No. 3 Mepps. I netted.

Louise is always full of go. Energy and enterprise took her down to the lower end of Scatterty, where she fished by herself whilst we were higher up the river, or on Montcoffer beat a mile or two downstream. Having the two beats meant plenty of fishing, but I had to drive the car between them from time to time throughout the day to check on the well-being of my charges. Consequently, Louise spent much of the day by herself, fishing carefully, keeping going, but not knowing quite what to expect as she had not yet caught a salmon. Leaving the car at the Scatterty fishing hut I walked down the river to find her standing at the water's edge looking frustrated. 'I've caught the bottom and it must be that soggy weed I've had before because the spoon is not stuck solid,' she said. She handed me the rod and I reeled up tight, felt a movement, then gave it back to her. 'It's a salmon. Play the fish yourself. I'll go down the bank with the net.' In this way, the salmon, a grilse, arrived at our feet upon the grass. 'The smallest one we've had this year,' I commented. Louise has not yet forgiven me for that remark – even after all these years. To her, it was the most wonderful fish, perfect in every way, glistening and shapely. The following day, on her own, she lost a salmon in Maggie Mill. This was just hard luck, for she couldn't reach the edge of the water, owing to a flooded reed bed, and therefore couldn't use the net. She managed to draw the fish, a larger one, onto the wet and flattened reeds, but the hook fell out and the salmon slithered back into the river.

The next day . . .

21 October. River Deveron. Montcoffer beat. The Craig. Gerry scored a first.
8 lb. Very fresh run. 2¹/₄-in. Brown & Gold metal Devon minnow. I netted.

Gerry has spent much time fishing in Chile where he picked up strange cries
from his boatman guide. His hollow cry echoed down the pool, and I looked up
to see Gerry prancing about as though someone had dropped a hot coal into his
boot – but the rod was bent into an exciting curve. A frightening responsibility
is thrust upon anyone who has the duty to net another's first salmon, and this
time the task was not easy. The water was fast and ran high through The Craig –
there was no backwater in which we could conclude the fight. In the end, Gerry
headed the fish upstream, ran it up for 10 or 12 yards, then turned the head
downstream and swam him straight into the net. It was a triumph for Gerry,
and a reward for me because I had spent some hours in Devon before the
holiday, making the best minnow mounts I could devise, and one of these had
done the trick.
    One day on . . .

22 October. River Deveron. Montcoffer beat. Mare's tail. 6 lb. Myself, 2¹/₄-in.
Brown & Gold Devon minnow.

There is little to say about this salmon. He came in high water and brought luck
with him. Skill played no part in the proceedings for there was little to indicate
where to fish in the rushing flow – just cast out, let the bait swing, reel in slowly
and hope. Unfortunately, Clive came away empty handed. He had skill,
humour, and the equipment, but despite his persistence he lacked a fair ration
of luck – the only fish he hooked came unstuck after a few heavy breathing
moments for us both above King Edward's Burn.
    There was then a break of several days in which the river flooded, the pupils
returned to the south, and I was joined for three final days by Bill, Tewdwr and
his son. The following entry records the only fish we caught.

30 October 1980. Scatterty. King Edward's Burn. Tewdwr had an 8-lb fish on
No. 4 upstream Mepps which he cast to the burn mouth. Played it and beached,
but the hooks broke and the fish fell back into the river. Bill then saw the salmon
lying under the bank taking a breather, and gaffed it. The combined age of these
two was 154 years.

The previous year, in 1979, we also fished the Deveron in the final days of the
season. On one of those, the 24 October, Bill and I took four salmon on the fly.
The weights were 4 lb, 8 lb, 14 lb and 16 lb. Two days earlier Bill had a fish of
14½ lb on a 1-in. Black Dart tube fly. Since designing the Black Dart it has been
used on many rivers with success: Dart and Deveron, Tamar, Test and others.
It is not a fly for low water, for it cannot be tied in a size shorter than one inch,

but it has my full confidence when there is a reasonable flow and some colour in the river. The dressing is to be found in my earlier book **Salmon and Sea Trout Fishing**.

The Survivor – a sea trout story

The will to live now left her, the driving urge slowed as she extruded the final pearly eggs into the stony bed of her spawning redd. With the last of them gone, fertilized by the shed milt of a small cock sea trout, she turned her empty flacid body to swim down river to the sea. White fungus covered her head, which was over-large for the thin, wasted body with a split and ragged tail. For a while she maintained direction downstream, moving a little faster than the current, but soon the water overtook her, rolled over the feebly swimming body and washed her down towards the sea. A fox who found the stranded fish ate the pale and tasteless flesh in the night, and the head he left was picked clean the next morning by crows and magpies. A raven watched the feast from high in the cold December sky but he did not descend because men were active close by, fixing a metal plate to a block of granite. The bronze plaque recorded the various names, important in their time, of those responsible for the completion of the dam, which would store the rains of winter and flood the valley in which the sea trout spawned. The impounded waters would meet the requirements of the citizens of a south Devon town during the dry weeks and months of summer.

The dam was closed, the waters rose covering a farm road and a bridge which crossed the sea trout stream. A place of beauty was re-created less beautiful than before. The river below the dam became a trickle of compensation water, the bed silted, bushes and weeds grew down the banks to choke the living soul of the stream, whose spiritual departure after some thousands of years was recorded on the metal plate.

Above the level of the enclosed waters the stream lived on. The sea trout eggs hatched in spring into tiny alevins, complete with a sustaining yolk sac. The little fishes grew slowly to a fingerling size and then were nourished meagrely by the pure waters of Dartmoor. These waters tumbled freely down to be impounded in the reservoir and the water pipes of the far-off town. The bright and shining sea trout fingerlings swam down the stream into the still waters above the dam where the newly-flooded ground provided rich feeding. Unaware of the life sentence imposed upon them in the reservoir by the mayor and corporation of the town, the fingerlings played freely in the morning sun which lit the ever-moving mirror of the surface waves above their heads. They chased each other in and out of the submerged granite walls of the abandoned farm and the hut circles of earlier Bronze-Age men. Their birthright, now taken from them, was to go down river to the sea and there feed well, grow fast and strong and then, in shining, muscular maturity, return once more to spawn in the river of their birth,

But with the passing of the months the numbers of this carefree band, who should by now have gone to sea, reduced – the heron took his toll along the water's edge in the early dawn, some just expired, and others were sucked to a black death in the mechanical contraptions of the dam.

Some of the peal fingerlings continued to grow in silver streamlined beauty, reaching sizes of 12 to 14 inches, to be caught on flies at the water's edge by startled brown-trout fishermen. When the west wind blew in winter the constant rains raised the level of the water and dark waves overflowed the dam to be transformed into white and silver pearls of spraying beauty falling 50 feet to the dam pool below. With these pearls went a solitary 10-inch peal, sole survivor of the earlier darting, flickering shoal of fish. Bruised and gasping he lay quietly on the bottom of the pool below the waterfall. His gills and mouth opened and closed slowly, absorbing the life-giving oxygen of the now well-aerated waters. Slowly, an awareness filled his being as strength returned and the magnet of the ocean reached him from the far-off sea.

Slipping out of the pool the survivor made his way down the trickling remnant of the ancestral river trail. Farther down the valley other streams joined the waterway, which grew in size and slowed somewhat in speed. Wild March daffodils lined the meadowy banks, dippers bobbed white waistcoats on the river rocks and woodpeckers flew in looping flight from rotten stump to hollow, rotting tree. The sea trout followed the gentler watercourse until his lonely body was welcomed by the healing arms of the sea.

For two years the peal followed the ocean currents of the North Atlantic. He grew muscular and strong. His tail changed from forked to square, his shoulders thickened and fat oozed between the pink flakes of his muscles. In June his milt sacs, now awakening with sperm, itched within his belly and he drove his 6-lb body irritably through the seas until, in the flicker of a moment, a water molecule fresh with the aromas of the Devon stream entered his mouth and once again the magnet pulled, this time for home as he entered the river through the estuary.

Eight miles up the river valley from the sand bars at its mouth, or seven as the cormorant flies, in the slumbering village of Buckland Magna, stood Buckland House, a Georgian home of unpretentious size with whitewashed walls, slate roof and stables gently rotting in disuse. The lawn of this house (a tennis court before the war, when gardeners were employed) sloped down to Monk's Pool on the river. The owner was a smallish man, a widower stooped and slow of movement, aged 80.

Snipe head

Arthritis so knobbled his fingers that he found it difficult to tie on his salmon and sea trout flies, not that he complained – it was just that these days they made the eyes of the flies so much smaller and the nylon thicker, or at any rate so it seemed.

The old man's pleasures were limited to his study, which looked over the lawn to the river, the company of his black labrador, Snuff, and, on his better days, to fishing for sea trout for an hour or two from dusk onwards. At times with the rod resting against the riverside bench he did not fish at all but just sat and waited and reminisced in the warm comfort of July evenings. The dog followed the example of his master, whom he guarded and loved with watchful eyes.

The old man's study comforted him during the day. Watercolours of birds were on the walls, a photograph of himself in Royal Flying Corps uniform with his Wings taped to the frame stood alongside one of his wife as a young woman in a cloche hat. Rods, binoculars, books, desk, chairs, all were there of right as well-tried friends. At a pine table against one wall of the study was a high stool and on the table a fly-tying vice, scissors, feathers, fur, silks and varnishes. This outfit had been given to him at Christmas by his daughter, but he was reluctant to make a start by following the instructions in the little book in case he found his fingers too infirm, or eyesight more dimmed by age than he would care to admit to himself. But the plunge had to be taken so, with decision, he sat on the stool, turned on the table lamp and fixed a No. 8 hook in the vice. A simple fly was the answer – just a silver body and a black wing, then he would have made a start. It proved to be easier than he had thought possible – the fly was just the right weight and size. It would work. Yes, there was no doubt it would be accepted by the peal – a good and simple fly. It was really very simple, he thought, and resolved to make another for his grandson who sometimes came to stay.

It seemed that it would never grow dark that evening as the old man sat on his bench beside Monk's Pool. His rod was set up, with the fly and nylon of his cast soaking in a little pool at the river's edge. He had seen three bats flit by –for as long as he could remember he had always waited to see three before judging it dark enough to start. Two bats were not enough, and to commence at the sight of one would mean such an early start that all the fish would be frightened. He must remember to tell his grandson about the bats. A proper boy, his grandson, fished for trout in the moorland burns and ate them for his breakfast. Yes, it was just the sort of thing the boy would like to know.

By Jove, that was a big peal. The old man heard a heavy splash and saw the widening waves where a great sea trout had jumped clear of the water and crashed down tail first. He rose, picked up his rod, crept forward, and slid softly down the bank in to the river. Three short casts he made, laying the line gently on the dark water. No splash, no noise, and then a quiet and steady pull as the Survivor took his fly. The old man raised his rod and slipped. . . . They found him next morning face down in the river, waders full, the rod clutched in stiffened fingers: there was no fly.

That evening Snuff sat alone beside the bench and whined from time to time. The old man's daughter saw a great sea trout jump several times when she came to fetch the dog to the house. Perhaps there was something wrong with the fish, but you could not see clearly. After all, there were bats about already.

CHAPTER 9

EPILOGUE

The spawning of salmon

If you visited the salmon spawning beds of the river Dart in October in low water the only fish you would see in the open shallows would be small brown trout. In that month I could show you salmon both upstream and downstream of these beds of little stones where they will lay their eggs, but they would be in holes, under rocks, in dark channels. They would be waiting, ripening and playing. That they play in October there is no doubt – I have seen them. There seems to be a light-heartedness which follows the end of the season. They cannot know the significance of the time, any more than the cock pheasant understands that the end of the shooting season is 31 January, but perhaps the mating time to come is the stimulus.

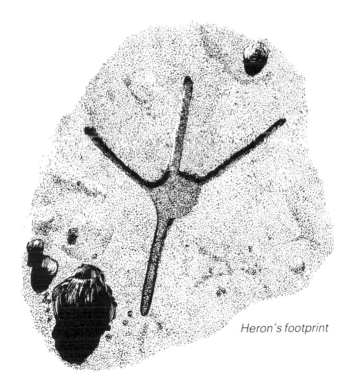

Heron's footprint

81 *A Dartmoor salmon spawning stream*

82 *The waves of water displaced by the cock fish as they chase off rivals wishing to attend a chosen hen* (6 December 1987)

83 *The dorsal fins of two salmon. 'Fourteen salmon passed within six feet of me: twelve of these went down, and only two went up.'* (13 December 1987)

84 *The scene had changed . . . one or two had died* (13 December 1987)

They seem to chase each other to determine a pecking order, for the cocks will be consumed by jealousy when the spawning weeks arrive. With guidance you could touch one of these fish on the tail, but only for a whisp of time, or you can lie full length, head propped on elbows, to see them swim beneath your rock. Each fin is visible and each is put to use as they hang motionless, drop back a foot, lift, sink or flee. The fins are lustrous and alive; they are different from the still, folded, lifeless skin and gristle fins of the dead salmon you have heaved upon the bank.

By the end of November and in December the salmon move to the shallow water covering areas of small stones. There you may see them, not unconcerned by your presence but more intent on their purpose and rivals than on you. The culmination of their being is at hand and with the need of fulfilment comes a carelessness.

On the morning of Sunday 6 December 1987 I watched a small hen fish deposit her ova in a redd she had scooped out with her tail. The small displaced stones were piled in an arc below her, making the trough she had cut lighter in colour than the surrounding river bed. From time to time her flank was curved by convulsions and she extruded her eggs – it seemed to me a rather rash affair as there appeared to be no cock close by to add his fertilizing milt.

With me on that morning was Julian Waterman who had come to record the granite-boulder-strewn isolation of Dartmoor for his drawings. Further down the valley we came on several salmon spawning in shallow water; our attention was drawn to the place by the noise of splashing, and the waves of water displaced by the cock fish as they chased off rivals wishing to attend a chosen hen. The slight depth of water over the small stones in which the hens had cut the redds was barely sufficient to cover the backs of the fish. Many dorsal fins cut through the surface skin of the river; sometimes their backs showed as a blackened curve, and their tails thrashed on air. Wherever the river bed was suitable and the water not too deep there were salmon spawning, fighting and fulfilling. Their excitement was catching and exhilarating; our fear of the possible annihilation of their race reduced as we witnessed their tenacious hold on life.

We saw mergansers fly up and down the valley, mallard too, and a group of confiding teal sprang from a hidden pool. It was a magic sunlit morning.

I returned on the following Sunday, the 13 December, and found the scene had changed. There was still an active pair or two, but the surging thrust, the vitality, had gone from the fish. They were tired. There was no doubt of their exhaustion. Gone were the chasing lunges of the males and the convulsions of the hens. One or two had died. The living swam slowly, and many moved downstream. I crept out onto a bank of gravel which stretched into the river and crouched there, kneeling, my legs and feet growing numb in the coldness of the water. For an hour I watched and during that time 14 salmon passed within six feet of me: 12 of these went down and only two went up. Several were diseased with white patches on their heads and bodies. The water was shallow in that place, forcing the salmon to cross the gravel bank with their dorsal fins exposed – I could have touched them with my thumbstick. It was a sad sight, for few would reach the healing waters of the sea, there to feed and grow strong again. When the rains came, as they did within the week, the survivors would disappear in the strong water, which would wash them down the valley. Few would be seen, many would be broken on the rocks and only one or two would reach the sea. In seven weeks, at the opening of the new season, one of these kelts might take my Devon minnow on the lower waters of the river. Such February kelts must be returned as their well-mended silver sides disguise a weak body.

On the moor in February and March, between the bedstones of the spawning areas, little-eyed alevins will hatch to renew the life cycle. Countless thousands of alevins, an infinite spread of tiny fish will survive the depredations of eels, feeding trout, the heron and the mink. They will go to sea two years hence, then return to the river of their birth after one or two sea-winters to become, in turn, the parents of the race.

Barn owl

Index